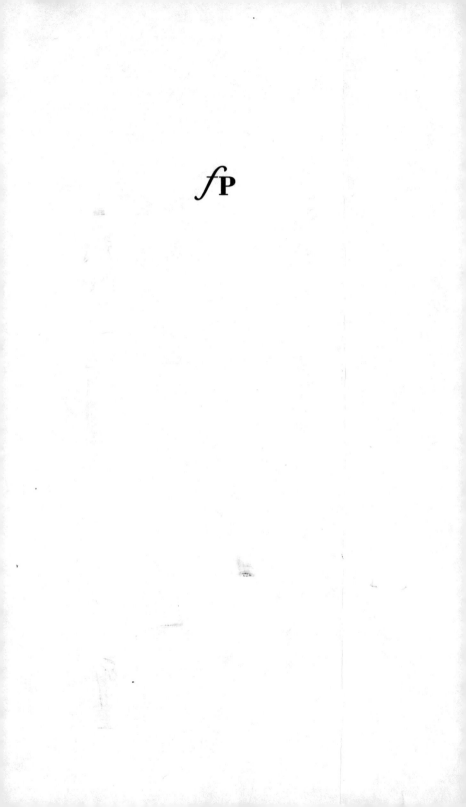

Ferocious Romance

What My Encounters

with the Right

Taught Me

About

Sex, God, and Fury

Donna Minkowitz

The Free Press

NEW YORK

*f*P

THE FREE PRESS
A Division of Simon & Schuster Inc.
1230 Avenue of the Americas
New York, NY 10020

THE FREE PRESS *and colophon are trademarks*
of Simon & Schuster Inc.

Designed by Jenny Dossin

Manufactured in the United States of America

1 3 5 7 9 10 8 6 4 2

Library of Congress Cataloging-in-Publication Data

Minkowitz, Donna, 1964–
    Ferocious romance : what my encounters with the right taught me
about sex, God, and fury / Donna Minkowitz.
      p. cm.
     1. Evangelicalism—United States. 2. Minkowitz, Donna, 1964–
3. Homosexuality—Religious aspects—Christianity. I. Title.
BV3773.M56 1998   98-28823   CIP
277.3'0829'092—dc21
[b]

ISBN 0-684-83322-0

Contents

A few names have been changed, but all the people in this book are real.

Acknowledgments

Randy Meadoff and Edward Ball were the Muses of this book, and contributed huge amounts of its genetic material. (I cannot thank them enough for their part in this baby.)

My smart, sensitive editor at the Free Press, Bruce Nichols, was a careful steward of this project from its inception. My agent, Jed Mattes, was hard-nosed and nurturing at once. I would also like to thank my mother for her love and support of me and this book.

Deb Tudor and Elizabeth McNamara gave me help far beyond the call of duty, and deserve riches. And the Saturday morning people were a literal revelation.

Gorgeous love also to Jane Shufer, Jill Weiner, Stephanie Smolinsky, Susan Minkowitz, Tina Minkowitz, Aldo Valmon, and Barbara Raab.

Finally, I would like to thank some of the religious-right people in these pages: Larry Burtoft, Bobby Ace, Paul Hetrick, Gary Oliver, and Laura Tucker. You rock my world. May you each find your way to Heaven.

DEDICATED WITH GREAT LOVE
TO EDWARD BALL AND RANDY MEADOFF

Ferocious Romance

The marriage of heaven and hell.

BLAKE

1

The Toronto Blessing

"He is offering you everlasting life, not membership in an institution!" the pastor shouts into a crowd of four hundred people, who scream back their defiance of all institutions and memberships therein. I knew I'd feel at home here, with people who cackle, ululate, and bray their praise of God. The Toronto Airport Christian Fellowship, one of the most popular religious-right churches in the world, has been kicked out of its own denomination for being too "extreme."

There's an excited, expectant atmosphere in the room, very much like at an early gay liberation meeting. A diffident young man walks up to the lectern and asks ardently whether any of us are here for the first time. We Toronto virgins raise our hands, and by doing so, get to feel like we're immediately participating in the life of the group. The man calls out countries, states, and provinces of origin, so we can stand and be clapped for being from wherever we are. Those who've been here a few days longer than the virgins are invited to participate in an even more direct way: "If there's anybody here that's been particularly touched by the Father lately and would like to testify," says the shy young man, "we need a few people."

I've come to Toronto because I like people this warm— ecstatic, extreme, and cheerily fey people, to be precise. My own people, gays and lesbians, have been known to get pretty ecstatic themselves; but I've also discovered that our alleged enemies, the religious right, like to go out of control and get crazy as much as we do. They just do it in their own way.

The way that the evangelicals' God was manifesting his extreme and disquieting self at the Canada airport sounded admirable and terrifying at once. There were magazine reports that, among other things, these people had "vomited in the Spirit," which sounded like a punk-rock version of evangelicalism. I had to see it.

The airport church lies in a dreary suburb of Toronto called Etobicoke, not far from the runways. Shining in a gray industrial park no one would visit for any other reason, burning perhaps dangerously close to the chemical plants and airline fuel reserves, the church's ecstasy has become a major source of passion (and contention) for evangelicals all over the world. Since the Holy Spirit began showing up regularly at services in 1994, more than a hundred thousand religious-right folks from America have visited the Toronto airport to acquire some of TACF's "fire."

It is perhaps not incidental that John Arnott, head pastor of TACF, is a former travel agent. Special deals have been arranged with nearly all the hotels and rental car companies at the Toronto airport so that people can combine a week's vacation with a pilgrimage to the church whose people come unbridled with the spirit of the Lord.

The denomination that kicked them out, the Association of Vineyard Churches, is itself considered "extreme"—at least by progressive critics of the religious right and by Christians (both progressive and conservative) who don't like to see too many miracles happening in church.

Many evangelicals fear the Toronto Blessing as much as progressives fear the religious right. "The power behind them . . . is demonic, not divine," read a pastor's typical letter in *Charisma* magazine, the journal of record for Pentecostals. Another letter called the Toronto churchgoers "immature and carnal."

As the diffident man speaks, two women are dancing by themselves in the wide side aisle. One, a flush-faced fiftysomething, looks a little mad, twirling a pink streamer and scampering lightly on her feet like some sort of ecstatic elf. The other is a vigorous, Gray Pantherish old woman in a T-shirt and painter's pants, who looks as though she's just come back from painting signs for a peace demonstration. The Gray Panther gestures rapidly with a baby blue triangular flag, as though she were an airport worker signaling to a plane. They both look crazy, but I sort of envy them. At different times in my life, I too have wanted to be inhabited by gods and dance ecstatically; what's happening in this church is what I prayed would happen to me as a teenager (although I was a Dionysian, not a Christian, and I prayed that the spirit would enter me through eros, or through drugs).

The Torontans constantly speak of God's anointing being on them, but if they take themselves too seriously, it doesn't show in how they dress. (I can't call them Torontonians, because so many of them have come from other towns.) The male pastors and most of the band are wearing jeans, and the women in the audience wear dresses and slacks in which they can move (a few of *them* even have on jeans). Standing in front of me is what appears to be a lesbian couple with their children, holding their palms out to God and shaking to His beat.

> "Step by step, we're getting stronger!
> Little by little, we're taking ground!
> Every prayer a powerful weapon!
> Strongholds come tumbling DOWN and DOWN
>   and DOWN and DOWN and DOWN!"

Everyone shouts on the *down*s. This song's a little frightening, but it's also—dare I say it?—empowering. The content is basically the same as that of the chants I've chanted at my favorite political demonstrations. The verses go like this:

> "We want to see Jesus lifted forward!
> We want to see Jesus lifted high!
> That all men might see the truth and know
> He is the way to heaven
>
> "We want to see—[*clap! clap! clap!*]
> We want to see—[*clap! clap! clap!*]
> We want to see Jesus lifted up!"

The Toronto worshippers talk and sing all the time about Jesus (and by extension, themselves) being "lifted up," and all their oppressors, who command the "strongholds," being cast down. Next the congregation sings another song about "Jesus . . . on a white horse" coming in to vanquish the people in power and claim the heavenly throne for *us*.

"Whoa . . . oh, oh, oh! [*hoofbeats!*]
Whoa . . . oh, oh, oh! [*hoofbeats!*]
He rides in majesty
Majesty, majesty
In majesty he rides."

A country ballad, it sounds a little like the Kenny Rogers song in which "the coward of the county" beats up all the men who've raped his girlfriend.

The new, gleaming church we're sitting in is the size of a rock-concert hall, and sunlight pours in from eight weirdly angled geometric windows, a strangely modern touch. A portion of the ceiling is mirrored so that we can watch ourselves being overcome, then raised. Long strips of red tape line the floor in a huge, empty area at the back of the hall, which I'm told will be used later when we get "slain in the spirit" and need a space for our eloquent bodies to fall.

As the music ends, three people from the audience rush up to testify. Linda Hinton, a young woman in a long denim jumper, tells how all her life she'd been plagued with "unforgiveness towards men." She doesn't say why, but that "it was very hard for me to talk to men, or even to look at them for more than two seconds." The formerly diffident announcer, a TACF staffer named John Busmo, by now has acquired the air of a confident TV game-show host: "So, would you say the Lord has set you free?"

She would. The next testifier, Vivian Ramspacher, also suffers from female troubles. "I just want to trust in the Lord, but part of me would always hold back. I would hold the stress in my stomach so that I couldn't eat very much." But at a service last Tuesday, Vivian, who's visiting from Richmond, Virginia, lay on the floor "and the Lord used me for two hours!" Since then, she says, her eating disorders have evaporated.

Busmo comments: "Often we see the Lord as being very similar to some of the key figures in our lives." Vivian couldn't trust in the Lord, he suggests, because she'd had so many unpleasant experiences with these "key figures," presumably in her family of origin. This transference can be resolved, the Toronto preachers say, when we realize that "our heavenly Daddy" is far superior to the earthly version that so many of us encountered.

Women testify at TACF much more frequently than men, but finally a man steps forward, Michael Petersmark of Pontiac, Michigan. Petersmark, a hearing man who is pastor of the Deaf Assembly Faith Church, begins signing and speaking at once: "I said, Yes, Lord, *take me away!* I want to be *with you!* Also, he showed me myself and that was not a very good-feeling experience. I saw his glory and my worthlessness." A large number of his parishioners from Pontiac are in the hall, in a large deaf section. As he

and Busmo pray for them—"Let deaf ears be opened!"—
the deaf men and women from Pontiac shriek aloud in
agony and make retching noises.

"Lift your hands and close your eyes, and God'll give
you a big surprise!" An ebullient, thirtyish black man
named Curtis is giving the sermon this evening, and he
begins with this risqué promise of a sainted kiss. Conservative as the airport church is on erotic matters, the idea of
sex with God figures implicitly—and sometimes even
explicitly—in its preachings. "My perception of Jesus was
this naked man hanging on a cross," Curtis says. "Did you
know he was naked on the cross? How many of you
would hang naked on a cross for me?"

The Torontans speak very harshly of fornication, but
they adore the idea of being ravished by God. Though they
eschew alcohol, they speak positively of spiritual "drunk-
enness" (the souvenir T-shirt for sale in the church bookstore shows a big anthropomorphized bunch of grapes
falling to the floor in a delightful stupor). Idiocy and insan-
ity are not far from their conception of holiness. "How
many of you know that the gospel is foolishness?" Curtis
asks us. At this, a woman erupts with hyena noises, and
some children begin crying out in the voices of other animals. The three who testified a moment ago are writhing
on the floor, having had hands laid on them by members
of the prayer team whose real duty is to open the mind to
just this sort of intoxication.

Women and men continue to make animal noises
throughout the sermon—sometimes quite distractingly—
and the Gray Panther and her friend return to their

exhibitionistic dancing in the side aisle. Later I will learn that the Gray Panther is a leading member of the prayer team, and the elf's prophecies have been recognized by senior pastor John Arnott as indubitably coming from God. For now, we all leave our seats and repair to the red lines at the back, where hundreds of us line up to be "prayed on" by certified TACF volunteers who have passed lengthy courses in inducing the spirit. "We have very few rules here," a pastor told us earlier in the evening, "but one of them is that you only let yourselves be prayed on by the people with the pink or blue badges. Blue dots mean they are authorized to pray for both male and female."

Many of the congregants have traveled thousands of miles just to participate in this ceremony. I watch as men, women, and children wait impatiently for a pink or blue badge to get to them so the Holy Spirit can connect and they can finally fall backwards. One stranger puts his hands on you from the front and one from the back, like some complicated sexual encounter. (These roles even have names that could be lifted from the gay male sex lexicon: "pray-ers" and "catchers.") It reminds me of the theater game called "trust," where you fall backward, hoping that your partner will agree to catch you. On the red strips, people begin falling over like dominoes. The ones who haven't been ministered to yet look on, forlorn and envious, like people waiting for a drug dealer, or a date who's blown them off.

"Just marinate in the Lord," members of the pink and blue team tell those who are already on their backs. "Just soak." Part of me would like to "marinate," but I've been on the wagon for so long. The action on the red strips is uncomfortably alluring, and I beat a hasty path to the exit.

℞

The second night, we sing an even fiercer hymn:

> "We will BREAK dividing walls [*we stamp our feet!*]
> We will BREAK dividing walls [*stamp!*]
> We will BREAK dividing walls
> In the name of Your son
>
> "We will BREAK dividing walls [*stamp!*]
> We will BREAK dividing walls [*stamp!*]
> And we will be one!"

The hymn's verses, sung to an Irish jiggy–sort. of melody, sound like a cross between a Nazi marching tune and a bathtub sex song:

> "Oh, there's a place of command and blessing
> Where beauty and harmony dwell
> A place where anointing oil is flowing
> Where we will be one
>
> "We will BREAK dividing walls! [*stamp!*] etc.
>
> "Oh, you have called us to be a body . . ."

So much of this church, it seems, is about simultaneously expressing the need to "be a body" and pour oil all over oneself and other people and the need to "BREAK" the things that inspire the body's rage. During testimony time tonight, Pat and Peter, a couple from northern Ontario, come up to share that previously, Peter had dominated Pat viciously. Standing before us, Pat is white-faced and silent, while Peter speaks authoritatively about his own domination. "I thought my wife was second class!" he says. "I thought she was secondary! I come from a very conservative, religious, Pharisaic background, and I thought that my wife should come second to me!" His arm contains her the whole time. Pat says no words, but her arms and legs shake violently, as though she were manifesting her rage at him through her entire body. The crowd cheers, identifying her jerks as a divine gift. After a while, the rigid Peter gets the shakes too, the ministry team prays energetically on them, and they both fall down.

Tonight's perky male announcer, standing over their prone bodies, calls out, "More, God! More! More! More, God!" and Pat and Peter convulse like epileptics.

One of the things I love about the Toronto Airport Christian Fellowship is its devoted attention to people who, as tonight's speaker puts it, "have so much anger and we don't know why, because of hurts of the past." "Our church has always catered primarily to misfits," church administrator Steve Long tells us later at a special session for visiting church leaders, "for example, people who had been sexually or physically abused." More and more churches, Long comments, "are recognizing that that's the reality of who comes to their services." Pat, tonight's abused wife, is speaking with her body in a way that's classic to traumatized people, especially women—

saying things with her spasming limbs that she apparently can't say to her husband through her open mouth. Yet this way of communicating is the very behavior the Torontans hold most sacred—a "manifestation," as they call it, of God's power, not of the unconscious attempting to speak. Roaring, shaking, falling, and even speaking in an unconscious manner are signs, for the Torontans, that God is in you, not signs that there may be something in you that wants to come out and can't.

If the services are full of testimonies from the traumatized—"He's been breaking all fear of man for me!" croons a typical testifier at a TACF women's conference—the shelves of the church bookstore are loaded down with books about sexual abuse, battering, and childhood violence. The bookstore has both *From Victim to Victor: A Biblical Guide to Turning Hurting into Healing*—which says it is "for anyone who has been victimized by trauma and abuse"—and *From Victim to Victory: Prescriptions from a Child Abuse Survivor.* (There is also a display for a book called *Adult Children and the Almighty.*) The store offers twenty-one books in all on this general subject, including thirteen specifically on sexual abuse and a few on the delicate subject of sexual abuse *by pastors.* Prominently displayed is a book called *Battered into Submission: The Tragedy of Wife Abuse in the Christian Home.* Whatever one can say about the Toronto leadership, they do not sugarcoat sexual or family violence, or deny its existence.

Instead, it appears, they worship it.

"Lord, we really need your fire tonight," says a heavyset, passionate, curly-haired woman singer with a British accent, introducing a song that sounds like what Melissa

Etheridge would sing if her cruelly rejecting lover were God. Called "Come with Your Fire," it invites the Lord to burn and devastate the singer because this "is the only means" by which the two can become close. (*"It's my heart's desire / To go through the fire / Because this is the only means, I gladly choose."*) As a symbol, the cross has always invited the worship of victimhood, but the Toronto worshippers take this to a further extreme than most, setting up their worship services so that the most traumatized are always the ones who appear most blessed.

Tiffany Bingham, an attractive young woman in a purple T-shirt, cheerily testifies: "A number of years ago my own father hurt me terribly. He just did so many things that really hurt my heart. I really cried out in pain because I was so broken. That's when I met Heavenly Daddy!" she exults. (*Broken*, in TACF-speak, is a *good* thing, much as *beat* was to the Beats. When you get beaten, Kerouac and these Christians think, you can get beatified.)

The announcer enthuses, "I see with Tiffany just an enormous depth of her relationship with her Daddy." He adds, a bit enviously: "And I really want some of that for myself!" Five members of the prayer team apparently feel the same way; they attach themselves to her like sucking remoras and don't let her go until she's staggering under their attentions.

All the testifiers tonight are female, and as the second woman steps up to tell about her back problems and the irregularities of her menstrual cycle, women in the audience begin crying out in pain. (I've never been in a church where women's minor ailments were discussed with such ardor. But these women, like the nineteenth-century hysterics, apparently invest so much of their pain in small physical symptoms that merely mentioning tense stomachs can feel like an avenue to the cross.) The third testifier, Sweetie Ties, from Ossining, New York, announces, "If they had lemon laws for children, they would have sent me back! You talk about alcohol running in families—well, in ours, it galloped!" (Rose, the woman with the irregular cycle, yells loudly at this.) "I didn't know what love was— I knew what control was. I became exposed to chemicals that gave me asthma and knee pain. I hadn't been able to work in five years—I was taking morphine. Plus, I had lupus."

But then "I started coming to renewal about a year ago, and I now know what it is to be loved. I now know what it is to love myself! I'm taking half as much medication as I was, and I'm walking!" Well, this beats all, but I'm moved for Sweetie Ties. I clap loudly. Okay, people to whom terrible things have happened often *do* talk about their troubles in comically annoying ways. If this church can get Sweetie to walk and halve her dose, more power to it.

Rose, on the floor now after being prayed on, is laughing as though she were drunk.

Announcer (winking): "It looks like something's happening to Rose!"

Rose (gaily): "I broke my pelvis in six places and this is the first time that I haven't had any pain!" She shakes her hips furiously on the floor in rhythm.

Announcer: "Run, Rose!"

Rose gets up and sprints back and forth ten times, very fast. I'm a bit giddy with this, but also disturbed, as though I'd glimpsed Jean-Martin Charcot's experiments on his hysterics. (Charcot, one of the forefathers of psychiatry, operated a famous asylum in which female patients only were exhibited for live shows.)

Unlike Charcot, however, the practitioners of the Toronto Blessing offer hysterics more than laboratory exercises and a perpetual stage. They offer passionate love to hysterics, misfits, and victims, and even to folks who identify just a little with these categories. "Jesus is radically in love with you," head pastor John Arnott writes in his book about the revival, *The Father's Blessing*. "Jesus wants a bride who loves Him with abandonment." Good works aren't what pleases God, Arnott adds: "being in love with Him pleases Him." Arnott, whom his own deputy, Steve Long, calls "a misfit," writes ardently about the difference between Martha and Mary, and how Mary was more prized by Jesus, because Martha "ran around . . . trying to get dinner ready" for the disciples while Mary was doing what was really important, "resting at the feet of Jesus . . . saying, 'Ahhhh . . . Jesus, you're wonderful.'"

Arnott can be a very seductive writer, picking out riffs that make me want to wash those feet with *my* hair, too. "How would you feel if you asked somebody to marry you and this was the reply: 'Yes. I'll marry you. But I do not want any of that emotional stuff. I do not like it when you put your arms around me or kiss me or that kind of thing. I just want to be practical. I will work for you, make money, take care of the house and the kids and everything else, but do not try to kiss me or be intimate with me.' . . . Is that what what you want in a spouse? . . . Doctrine is not a substitute for a love affair." This isn't the way most people expect the religious right to talk about God—or about anything. But the Pentecostals and charismatics who comprise a near majority of the religious right often speak of God in such gorgeously romantic terms, as though all the sexuality in the world had been compressed into the relationship between God and believer.

The way they do it at the Toronto Airport Christian Fellowship sometimes makes me want to pack my bags and relocate to Toronto permanently, with a warm smile on my mouth and a big bouquet of roses for the Lord. At an Intercessory Prayer session in the middle of the day, Shirley, the dervish and Gray Panther, "sings in the spirit" for us, speaking in the character of God, in a minor key: "Do you know how much I love you? Do you know the extent of my love for you? I feel all your pain, I take it upon me. Will you allow me to love you?" This crazy lady has brought tears to my eyes. She continues: "I will forgive you, as I promised. I will restore you. . . ." The melody is a haunting sort of half-operatic, half-Asian aria and drone. It wakens in me barely acknowledged desires to be loved, forgiven, embraced entirely.

The Toronto Blessing is the other side of the conservative evangelical movement's well-known fixation on hellfire and damnation. Hundreds of thousands of believers fly to Toronto each year because the Torontans talk about what you will get if you're *not* damned: the parental love of God forever, unlimited and intoxicating. The mother who never pulls back; the father who never deprives you of him, ever. The lover who will chain himself for you, and never leave. The lover who will give whatever you need, even his blood.

Ferocious Romance

The "spiritually drunk" Torontans speak of Christ's
blood as though it were a never-ending fountain of mother's
milk. Reasons I would go to this church include: the special
"pastoral soaking party" once a month, where, Steve Long
says, all the volunteer and paid ministers "just have a lot of
desserts and pray on each other" till they get giddy; the gaily
colored "prayer streamers" for sale in the bookstore, long
beautiful ribbons for worshippers to dance with, in adult
and children's sizes; a Nova Scotia woman's testimony of a
vision she had in which she was an eight-year-old girl in pig-
tails, and Jesus grabbed her hand and skipped with her and
told her, "I am as thrilled with you as you are with Me";
and, especially, John Arnott's conversation with God in
which God confessed to him, "Oh, John, I just want to
wash your feet."

The Torontans often render God as a beautiful masochist whose superlative and almost unbelievable offer can
hardly be refused—die for me? wash my feet? let me hang
you up by nails for *how* long? It is no accident that his
redemptive body, for them, takes the form of pastry.

On my third night, I can hardly hold back any longer.
When Arnott, a fat man with a menacing air, calls on the
unsaved to step down to the front of the room, I step. It's
a little awe inspiring to be right up there at the center of
things, the axis of four hundred people's love and the focal
point for the attentions of the furnace-hearted ministry
team. The pink-and-blues always occupy the first two
rows so they can minister to all the insufficiently loved
ones who step up.

When I get up from my seat, Curtis is excitedly telling
us that we're not good enough for God and should by

rights be rejected, "because His standard is absolute per-fection! Jesus was the only man who ever walked the earth who fully satisfied God!" ("I don't understand that, do you?" Curtis asks later. "Why would God love *us?*") Love and repulsion intertwine in this story; Curtis next talks graphically about how physically disgusting Jesus became for our sake—"It says in the Bible, his appearance was so disfigured, beyond that of any man"—and how, stretched on the cross, he turned into a fetid "snake" because of his love. The message in my ears as I approach the altar is that Jesus got nasty for me—who am already too nasty for God—so that I can have God's love after all, even though, apparently, I don't deserve it.

God knows I want to be loved. It's nice, in the end, when an older woman lays her hand gently on my upper back and tells me I am unconditionally loved. There's a whole row of us, mostly young men, who've come down to the altar for a dose of lovin'. I am the only one who's accepting Jesus for the first time; the others are backsliders. Strangely, I start to feel a profound *shaking* in my chest, and if I were one of the Torontans, I'd be sure it was the Holy Spirit knocking. But I know it's not, because I haven't *really* accepted Jesus, and if the Spirit thinks I have, it's dumb. (Later, reenacting the scene with my sister, a physician, I discover that being touched that way on that part of the back can make you feel an exciting sort of *quaking* in your chest when you breathe.)

Hamming it up, I fall to my knees, and eventually on my face. The Torontans throw a traditional charismatic mod-esty-scarf over my bare legs, and John Arnott himself appears and scoops me up, putting his hands on my face and asking my name. It is nice to be touched this way by the chief minister. They gently pull me to my feet and lead me to a special indoctrination-session for converts in another room.

Inside the backstage room for new believers, things are much more tense. My companions, all in their teens and twenties, stare at their feet in shame and overwhelming sadness. I'm perplexed. I thought we could be happy now, or at least feel as though we were out of the woods. But our guide, the woman from New Life Ministries we followed in here, sweeps all those notions away.

"Now I'm going to tell you the meaning of what you just committed yourselves to!" Her air is that of a yuppie lawyer about to inform us that we had signed something really stupid, and she'll profit from it. "You have just signed a contract with God. And just like if you rented and had a landlord who owned your apartment, He is your lord. *He owns you now!* . . . You have been bought and paid for."

It's not fun to be told you have been purchased, but it gets even less thrilling when the program changes to that of a rigorous final exam. We are asked whether we're sure we'd go to heaven if we died, and if we're not sure, "and God asked you why you deserved it, what would you tell him?" Everyone answers satisfactorily except for one very sad young woman, who is ushered with me, the Spiritual Infant, to a sort of remediation session.

It's a reading-comprehension lesson. We're given two pamphlets; like so many pairs in Christianity, one is sweet and the other is disgusting. The sweet one asks *Who Am I?* and answers with biblical quotes grouped in three sections: *I Am Accepted; I Am Secure; I Am Significant.* The quotes say things like these: *"I am God's child."* . . . *"I am Christ's friend."* . . . *"I have been adopted as God's child."* . . . *"I am a saint."* . . . *"I am free from condemnation."* . . . *"I have been chosen and appointed to bear fruit."* . . . *"I cannot be separated from the love of God."* The other one, put out by Billy Graham's organization, teaches by means of many little drawings, all captioned this way: *People* (sinful). *God* (holy). The same drawing, of the gross *People* and the wonderful *God,* appears on every other page of the pamphlet. They are separated by an enormous chasm, because "we chose to disobey God and go our own willful way." The final drawing depicts *People* ("Sin Rebellion Separation") and *God* ("Peace Forgiveness Abundant Life Eternal Life"). The only thing that can bridge the chasm of our unworthiness is Christ.

The young lawyerly woman makes sure that we understand each of the drawings. Then she makes us sign commitments to God and Christ. Finally, detention's over. "You are released to go," she says. I'm surprised to feel a surge of affection as I prepare to take my leave of this rigid young woman. I hug her hard, and her mouth finally betrays a little warmth. Being bought and paid for is romantic to many people, I remember as I clutch my tiny souvenir copy of the Gospel of John—even, at times, to me. I guess in her own way she was only offering me love.

But ultimately, love isn't the main emotion expressed by the Toronto worshippers when God takes them over. I see the Torontans' view of God more fully when I begin to see my first prophecies at their services. One night, a woman in her thirties, alternately cringing and commanding, grants this Word to us: "He's giving us a hole, a vacuum, that can never be filled with anything but Him! We can't trust ourselves, but we can trust Him!" There is a big response from the congregation. Several make noises as if they were defecating or throwing up. Others howl as though they were giving birth. There is something liberating about these noises, unsettling as they are. They sound like an ill or angry people finally realizing that they are angry or ill, and expressing it. It's hard to listen to, but there is nothing put on about it. I'm sure these sounds express the way these people really feel, and that in itself makes this sickening spectacle moving.

John Arnott's response is also strong. He calls for "those who have a prophetic edge—especially those who've regularly been getting the Word of God at our services—to come up here" to the front and say more things that are on God's mind. Thirty or forty prophets come up—mostly women—and eight or nine of them speak to us in a row.

These prophets combine Elizabethan phrasing with contemporary slang. "I charge you not to be flaky," says the first, "cause we're not into bogus prophecy." The next woman, breathing hard, tells us to "Open your hearts, because there is something coming that is FAR BEYOND THESE WALLS AND FAR BEYOND THIS CITY, it's far beyond anything we've seen!" She sounds terrified. The people in the congregation scream as though they were in pain.

Most of the images in God's brain are military. A forty-year-old woman tells us, "I just keep hearing over and over again, 'When we hear the sound of marching in the mulberry trees, be ready!'" Armies, swords, and even donkeys to carry God's swordsmen figure in these fantastic, super-heated visions—along with a reference to the movie *Braveheart*. ("Just like in the movie, the sword was five feet long! You need to be on horseback to wield it.") Men and women cry out "Ho!" throughout the prophecy-time as though they were in the army of the Roman Empire. It looks like fun to wave imaginary weapons and babble in this way, about these things: "The church is like a womb! Take up the sword! Protect the womb! We have to have a sword in our hands to protect the womb of the baby!"

The fantasies are a romp, but the most important numbers are a little too intense to be called "fun." Before giving the major prophecy of the evening, Arnott's wife, Carol, nearly crumples to the floor until he forces her to stand. Trembling in his arms, pinioned in their bulk, she tells us: "It's a fire over us—burning the church—burning the people. *It is not the good fire! It is a consuming fire!* We're not gonna get away with—what we got away with before! Oh God! God's calling for a pure bride! We cannot pour out this anointing on a bride that's full of spots and full of pride and full of jealousy!" As God, she offers a final chance for reprieve, but warns: "But if you do not come to my gentle hand, the fire that is coming WILL . . . CONSUME . . . YOU!"

Almost all the prophecies speak of a terrible punishment that awaits. Hearing them, it's often hard to figure out whether it awaits us or our enemies. Depending on whether the prophet is speaking in God's voice or the voice of a quaking believer, the Word of God comes across as either rageful or masochistic. Which amounts to much the same thing. Hearing Carol refer to herself as a "bride full of spots" in one sentence and the bearer of a nasty fire in the next, I hear the same viscous, obscure sentiment in her speech. It is masochism *as* rage—murky, undivided, powerful.

In TACF's prophecies, "He [is] venting His anger and His fury through His people," John Arnott writes. "[We are] explosively displaying God's wrath." In church, he prays, "Let this city be blasted. . . . Ninety-five percent of the people here are controlled by the Enemy!" "You're gonna send your people out to look for those buzzards and shoot them down!" visiting preacherwoman Pat Cocking informs God at a conference for women. Mary Audrey Raycroft, a TACF pastor like an iron rod, gleefully relates a vision she had of "lassoing" "rebellious" Christians and branding them with a hot iron—"B for Betrothed!" These people think one of the earliest indications that the Holy Spirit was here was when a reserved Chinese pastor visiting in 1994 zipped around the church aisles like a lion "pouncing at people, claws out, roaring in their faces."

The Torontans celebrate victims in precisely the way that Christ did. And they ultimately worship His ambiguous rage, the rage of the victim.

"Six hours of bleeding, suffering agony," Arnott says with relish, as though he were describing a sexual fantasy.

"Every time he tried to breathe, he's working his wounds, so the blood cannot clot. So all his blood would pour out. He literally bled to death!" Arnott tells us it was necessary that Christ's death be as bloody, "horrible," and "torturous" as possible, so that God had "a legal basis" for forgiveness. "'When I see that blood,' God said, 'I'll *pass over* you!'"

There is a strange logic to this "merciful" crucifixion story that is rarely commented upon—the idea that Christ's torture can "pay for" anyone else's violation, that one act of torment can somehow redeem another. Even less merciful is the idea that an additional act of torment is *necessary* to redeem the first. In her book *The Origin of Satan*, religion historian Elaine Pagels explicates the bewildering duality that has always existed within Christian tradition between punishment and forgiveness, sadism and compassion. She suggests that the increasingly savage theological threats against "sinners" and "son of hell" in the New Testament have to do with the historical experiences of the writers of those works—persecution, starvation, torture, and martyrdom. As a religion of victims, literally created and promulgated by people who had been tortured and abused, Christianity contains an understandable vein of sadistic anger that is hardly ever acknowledged by its adherents.

This contradiction pervades the New Testament—the startling leap from "Love your enemies" to "Depart from me, ye cursed, into everlasting fire," the gaping chasm between "There must be no limit to your goodness, as your heavenly Father's goodness knows no bounds" and "It is a terrible thing to fall into the hands of the living

God." For the Torontans, it is the leap between God's unstinting, almost masochistic love (I will hang naked on a cross for you and deny you nothing, not even my blood) and his equally boundaryless and unquenchable hate (I "WILL CONSUME YOU!"). My entire time in Toronto, I am overwhelmed by the difference between the God who gets me drunk and gives me pastries and the God who wants to throw me down on the floor, terrified, until I realize that they are one and the same. To the Airport Christian Fellowship, love *is* rage.

"All the goals and ambitions of your life are fading from view," Arnott preaches, "because He's putting a brand, a mark upon you!" The branding that makes the Toronto pilgrims writhe on the floor and cry in pain and fear is the same branding that indicates God's ardor for them, and his sexual embraces. It is frightening, but then again, many people find love and sex pretty frightening in their own right. "Some of you are sitting there worried that you'll get burned alive!" Arnott tells the audience during the prophecy portion. "Wouldn't it be something if church would be a dangerous place to go into? Well, it is dangerous! Yes, it is dangerous! That fire that we speak of is real, and sometimes there are accidents!"

For the adherents of the Toronto Blessing, love always comes coupled with the sense of their intrinsic repulsiveness and undeservingness, and it always comes coupled with violence. They constantly seek reiterations of this contradictory thing they prize: fiery love, frightening sex, nurturing danger, as though the drumbeat of rageful loving were like the hit of a powerful drug. "Hit me, God!" Rhonda Carrington from Shreveport, Louisiana, testifies about telling Him. "Okay, God, hit me!" She was jealous because her husband had gotten the jerks and she hadn't. "He's saying He's got value for you, and the value is not so much in you—it's in Him!" the pastor laughingly tells her.

It is chilling to listen to them. But their furious services give them a way to bring their darkest, least acceptable emotions into the light of day. Writing about a neo-Pentecostal revival that once broke out at Yale, psychoanalyst Julius Laffal said: "By the fact of verbalization, glossolalia brings close to consciousness what the individual cannot put into words. Since the specific social tokens are lacking, the shame, guilt, despair or anxiety that might accompany [the unspeakable content] are avoided while the person feels that he has expressed the ineffable."

And rendered it holy.

For them, the most holy thing emerges from the least holy—that is the vastness of the act of transmogrification they are pulling off. That is why they must be inarticulate, though loud. "I want to pull a cork out of your MOUTH!" Mary Audrey Raycroft, strangely sexy and aggressive, suddenly shouts to the women's conference.

She makes me think of a parable from the gnostic Gospel of Thomas, written in the second century A.D. In the parable, Jesus asks three disciples to articulate what he "is like." Responds Simon Peter, "You are like a righteous angel." Matthew says, "You are like a wise philosopher." But Thomas says, "Master, my mouth is wholly incapable of saying what you are like."

Jesus responds—in pure Toronto airport fashion—"I am not your master. Because you have drunk, you have become intoxicated from the bubbling spring which I have measured out." To reward Thomas for becoming intoxicated (!), Jesus takes him aside and tells him "three things." When Simon Peter and Matthew ask Thomas what Jesus has revealed to him, Thomas says: "If I tell you one of the things which he told me, you will pick up stones and throw them at me; a fire will come out of the stones and burn you up."

How do the Torontans speak the things that can't be spoken without burning? By speaking them without words, and almost, without thoughts. They have to tremble and bleat because it is difficult to find a way to speak about being violated that does not take such form. Only speaking with their bodies makes it possible for them to worship at all. Only ecstasy, with its unspoken pain, will ever make them feel that they have any kind of soul.

2

Fire from Heaven

I am wearing a gray tweed jacket and twirling around on the grass by the centers of power. It's an October Monday morning, but none of us are going to work. We are going, very seriously, to play. I am twenty-three years old and feeling at one with sex, joy, wildness, beauty, freedom, letting the soft rain fall on me in front of the Capitol. It is the March on Washington for Lesbian and Gay Rights, only the second such event in history; I was too young to attend the first. I feel like I'm attending my baptism. Everything feels incredibly new on the dewy, hopeful grass next to the fat Smithsonian. We are here to conjure something that has barely even been imagined.

Love without inequality. Pleasure without restriction. Vulnerability without exploitation. To me, to most of us, gay love means all these things and more—an ecstatic knowledge, almost a *gnosis*, that sex is possible outside of the horrifying thickets in which the rest of the culture has hedged it. And that we ourselves can get to it! Visions of a totally satisfying oral bliss, what Ginsberg called "caresses of Atlantic and Caribbean love," the mind-stealing kisses of "human seraphim," a physical joy beyond the bounds of anything most people experience, almost beyond the bounds of desire itself, my God! no wonder people fear us! But they should not fear. They should open to the Ultimate, as we have done.

We've come as messengers, bringing our tender polymorphous perversity to the sexless Capitol and the sterile White House. Other movements are about violence, but our movement's sole goal is increasing pleasure and joy. Reagan lives inside this White House—it is 1987—but we know our movement could touch even him with its liberating wand and free his sexuality, his bad parenting, his crabbed life with Nancy. In our angelic attitude toward our mission here, we are direct descendents of the flower children who came here almost twenty years ago.

In my tweed jacket, I feel elegantly butch, like Radclyffe Hall on her way to her tobacconist's. This is a movement that celebrates anarchy, but I am one of its leaders. That's just one of the paradoxes that make the gay movement the sweet impossibility it is. I've brought a busload of women from my feminist karate school down here; I am the "bus captain," and the title makes me feel like a gentle but masterly authority figure, in control but also nurturing, just like the radical lesbian I am supposed to be. In my dojo, we believe you can have wildness and order simultaneously. Like most of the people at this march, we are looking for an integration of the contradictions that stunt human lives: strength and openness, male self-care and female caring, autonomy and love. We don't believe these attributes must be kept separate, as the rest of this culture seems to. The people at this march, proud young men in

dresses and mothers who fix cars and peanut butter sand-
wiches, see themselves as a new sort of people, people the
way people were meant to be: neither toadying or bully-
ing, selfish or self-sacrificing, destructive to themselves or
destructive to others—in the most profound and liberating
sense, neither male nor female.

To me, they seem like the children of paradise.

Unlike the rest of the country, we tell each other, homosexuals believe in a pleasure without victims. Most of my
friends from karate school are enthusiastic about non-
monogamy, and even more enthusiastic about the idea that
lesbians might someday have venues for happy anony-
mous sex, the same way gay men do now. We do not
believe that pleasure intrinsically wrongs people unless it is
contained. For now, we are content to flirt in the small
sweaty space where we take off our *gi*'s, as though we
were gay men rubbing elbows in the gym showers. The
atmosphere on the karate floor and on the bus to Washington, too, is very sexualized, as though we believed that
sex was a sort of sacred perfume that we needed to atom-
ize to make a place holy.

In the same vein, New Age people burn sage to drive away
bad energies. But our method seems to work. Feeling—
suddenly—wildly attractive in my rain-soaked clothes, I look
around at all the other marchers standing close to me and I
can tell that they believe it, too. There are slight Midwestern
boys blossoming under the blushing gaze of textile heirs,
strong-jawed women gently touching soft James Dean girls
with one finger, Puerto Rican guys in dancing boots finding
each other irresistible. It is as though sex is the singular
magic essence that can take all social barriers down, inte-

grate the warring elements in our characters, plunge us beyond all merely human boundaries. It has already taken us beyond the boundaries of decency, of legal rights, of social and sometimes physical safety. No wonder we would follow it anywhere. It is a powerful god to have on our side, and it loves us for being such ardent communicants. "Being a sexual people is our gift to the world," says one of our foremost sexual theorists, Joan Nestle.

As my fellow karate students and I march up Pennsylvania Avenue, a woman comes flying out from the sidelines to us. She is a retired Army officer in full uniform, in her fifties, and she kisses me on the lips in sudden warmth and passion. My buddies look at me with envy, but I feel transported. I was right: The gay and lesbian movement *is* the locus of the body's sacred fire, its ability to touch the entire universe. Its ability to connect with others at any and all times. There is something mystical about the fact that this soldier and I can kiss with no knowledge of each other whatsoever but that we are fellow human beings. It's like sharing food, or God's word, in a war zone.

❧

Perhaps it's especially me who feels like I am in a war zone. I haven't had sex with anybody in six years—since my high school girlfriend broke up with me. Perhaps it is partly for this reason that I've come to see eros as unconditionally revolutionary and transformative. Except for this kiss, it has been an item of deprivation and abstraction for me all this while, and therefore particularly easy to reverence. After this march, I will enter the erotic fray again (and again, and again) and I will write only about sexual issues. Every time I go to bed with someone, I will feel that I am serving the only God I know. I will feel I'm no longer an infidel, trying to pretend that any other sort of endeavor makes life meaningful. Meeting another person between the sheets, the only place that people really open fully to each other, I will feel I am letting them see the only godlike part of me, the part that compensates for everything that discomfits me.

No one reveals their core, outside of sex. I believe I have been hiding my realest self and talking only to other hiders, for six years. Out of that place of emptiness and concealment, I come back to sex at last as though I were participating in an altar call. A sharp-tongued but good-humored woman from karate school helps me break my long sexual fast. "Coming inland," Ursula Le Guin calls it, and it feels like that to me—no longer stranded like a wracked ship. Returning from exile.

As I get together with Catherine, I feel as if I'm leaving a place of salt and painful withering for the only garden that exists. "By the waters of Babylon, we lay down and wept, when we remembered Zion," I have read to myself so often in these years, and "How long, oh Lord, wilt thou quite forget me? How long wilt thou hide thy face from me?" Finally, he has stopped forgetting me. ("He," I suppose, is the god of communion with the other. Though you could say that *every* conception of God is ultimately about that—our hectic relation with all that is not ourselves.) Catherine and I get together after I ask her to spar with me at a party; that tiny bit of ritual violence makes it easier for me to caress and give pleasure to another person after so many years. For I'm scared to be once again seeing another person's exposed fire. Catherine's is frightening, passionate, and exuberant, and I'm not at all sure that I want to see it.

I pretend I do. Her kisses really are like being in a garden. And she moves her hips against me unconsciously whenever we touch! She kisses me whenever we enter a subway car, and it feels like I am definitely chosen and in the Kingdom. I am the property of the Lord of beautiful sensations and I will have them even in the dirt and bleakness of the subway. I feel intimately connected to Catherine from the moment she calls my name in bed. And she claims that I'm the sexiest woman in New York City.

I am a child of God. Finally I know it. Though I am slightly jealous that Catherine may be experiencing more of his ecstasy than I am. "Hit me, Sex, hit me," I want to say, but I decide that God will shower his blessings on me when and how he wants to. It is more seemly for me to be thankful for whatever delights I feel with my startled mouth whenever Catherine kisses me (I feel like I am tasting fruits of many different kinds), whatever moans He pulls from me when my knees start to fold and I am Disrupted in such a beautiful way on Catherine's bed.

She's fond of kissing me in public, as though she were inescapably driven to it, and that is possibly what I like most about Catherine—the aura of being driven. She likes the rabid way I spar, even though it's very unwise by karate standards. "You're deeply angry," she says, laughing. I don't care. I'm beginning to decide that anger's an important component of my eroticism. I don't care if it's not in the karate handbook. Right around the time that I hook up with Catherine, the women's movement has finally come to the world-shaking decision that sex can be utopian even when it looks most reactionary—maybe even *especially* when it looks most reactionary. Fantasizing cruel things while having sex is *liberating,* not harmful— because it sets free the cruel inner being within. Lesbians mostly concur. With the approval of our political movements, Catherine holds my wrists down while she's fucking me and I feel like I have finally come before the Almighty and out the brittle doors of the world.

It's on the floor before his blinding Throne that I make my residence now.

Is ecstasy about being *in* the body or *outside of* the body? I can't tell, but its radical indeterminacy frightens me, even though I seek it out over and over again. Is it about fully being in the present moment, or about *shattering* time and sense-experience? I'm a committed materialist, but I suspect that what I love about what sex does to me is that it takes me temporarily from the world of matter. It busts me out of prison! But if it's the physical I worship, why do I think the world's a prison?

I feel back in prison again when Catherine breaks up with me a month later. I have no sexuality left to me now—she's taken all of it with her. I feel like a fraud, writing about gay liberation when no one is touching me. I am not having sex so I wonder why I am allowed to remain in the order.

I feel shame whenever I'm not having sex, like someone who's unworthy of the right to touch His hand. But I go back to sex. I keep going back, and grace comes to me.

Each successive partner is a new redeemer. My grossest saviour, a woman whose mind and body repulse me, is like Jesus inhabiting a wretched human body for our sake. I feel gifted that I can find even her repulsiveness sexy; I can transmute anything into the holy.

No one else who I sleep with is repulsive. But I do find that I'm open to anyone who asks. Utterly and unconditionally open, like one of the temple prostitutes Paul was always terrified the early Christians were turning into. Eager to bear God's seed in any form—as once, in Toronto, I heard a dozen women yell that they were "pregnant with God" because they'd turned their bodies over to Him, holding back not a particle of eager flesh. But *I'm* more devout than they are, because I'm more than just open. If anybody wants me, I *need* with every part of my being to be in their arms. I feel I will die if I don't. How do I get infected so easily by their passion, so that their lust transfers itself over to me in a heartbeat? Because they become God to me as soon as they desire me.

Nancy, on the bus to the Persian Gulf War demonstration, bursting with muscles, touching me almost from the moment we meet. Ricki, selling me bread at the bakery, asking me home to dinner. At her house, I cannot do otherwise than seduce her. It's my job. Darcy from my French class, whom I'm not attracted to. Jean, who makes love to me as though she were drilling through granite. I need them all from the moment they lay eyes on me.

For the other piece of this, of course, is love. The comfort of Catherine's fingers in me is so enormous that I *know* all my needs will be filled. It's a sign. Cosmic shorthand, like God's messages to the Torontans about the marching in the mulberry trees. It's impossible for me to have sex without feeling I'm in love, just as it's impossible for the Torontans to go into spasm without knowing it's a sign that God loves *them*. When He throws me on the floor I just know that He would give me anything. When they touch me I know that they care for me with the care that a Shepherd feels for His sheep, or a parent for her infant, helpless the same way that I get helpless in sex.

ᗞ

All the time that I am following this creed, I take sex as a sign of radical disobedience. Though I believe I'm obeying the Sublime One when I have sex, I also feel intensely that I'm fighting back, that each caress is a blow of sorts. But who is it a blow *against*? It is a whack at all the forces that want to deprive me, want me to be untouched, unpetted, caged in. I understand these forces in political terms, as the social interests that don't want women, or lesbians, or people in general to feel sexual ecstasy. There certainly are social forces that ache to lace us up, but it's odd that I should identify them with the forces in my own head that want to shield me, hold me back. Unlike the religious right, I feel ashamed, "bad," sick, and unworthy when I *don't* have sex, not when I have it. Fucking makes me feel righteous.

And saying the word *fucking* makes me feel righteous beyond belief. I love disobedience as much as I love sex itself, the rebel-god who topples earthly rulers. Sexual chaos fights the "principalities and powers" St. Paul warned about, "the rulers of the darkness of this age, the spiritual hosts of wickedness in the heavenly places." Religious-right people love this verse and quote it all the time because at bottom their religion is, like mine, a Manichaean one. Both I and they believe it's Satan who controls this world.

The being that likes deprivation and hates pleasure is the master of this place. We both think so, even though the right prefers to take its pleasures through other means than merely bodily sex. We have to say no to this Controller! It's our duty, whether on the gay left or the religious right, because he hates God and smashes everything that brings us joy.

My sex has lots of rage in it because Satan has stepped in to choke it off. I will not let him! There's so much that I want to experience and I'm not going to let him gag me! I want to pull the cork out, I'm going to let out all the fire, if I have to storm police barricades to do it!

$\rightarrow$

"The goddess on the mountain*top*. Was burning in a silver flame. The sovereign of beauty and love. And Venus was her name." Ten years later, one of my favorite songs lilts from the speakers in a pretty auditorium at NYU Law School, where a group after my own heart is holding a teach-in for the uninitiated. In the intervening years, I've transformed myself into a bona fide "sex radical." But it hasn't been a decade of twirling around on the grass, feeling the untainted dew. Like me, the most radical thinkers in gay activism have long since decided that sex is *dystopian*, not utopian, to be worshipped not because it elevates us, but because it draws us gloriously down.

Shocking Blue's soft hymn to Venus notwithstanding, the sex god we now worship is an angry god. Those who seek to restrain sexual desire "do so because theirs is weak enough to be restrained," we sneer at abstainers and would-be edifiers like William Bennett; but we see ourselves, queer people and other sex radicals, as a breed of Nietzschean Supermen, brought here to fight petty conceptions of morality and crush the would-be stiflers of the id. Sex Panic!, the group behind this forum, sees sex as a door to all the disowned, most recalcitrant, most discomfiting parts of the soul.

The idea has a Luciferian tinge to it. "May you find wonderful things in the darkness," the most brilliant mind in sex radicalism, Pat Califia, once printed on her Christmas cards. Sex Panic! defends every kind of sex that has been castigated as "dangerous," "antisocial," and "nonnormative." It is the strongest champion of the individual will since Blake wrote "Sooner murder an infant in its cradle than nurse unacted desires."

Walking into NYU Law School, I expect to see a sex scene from Hieronymus Bosch—people masturbating over dead babies, maybe. But what I see once inside the pearly white gates is almost an anti-Bosch picture—a vision of the id as innocence itself, the very thing I was looking for in Washington. This beautiful assembly hall is filled with balloons painted all colors of the rainbow, as if children had finger painted them, and shaped like sweet little curves, gently flexed phalluses, endearing olives daubed with green. This is sex as pure play, childlike pleasure, capable of hurting no one, any more than delicious candy hurts, or splashing and being splashed in a pool. There are also giant beach balls that make me smile when the audience begins batting them around. The last two times I saw beach balls batted around in this puppylike way were at the Republican convention in Houston and at a Christian right men's conference in the South.

It was fun those times, too.

But in NYU Law School, as an added attraction, the speakers are belting out my favorite disco anthem: *"I'm your Venus! I'm the fire! at your desire!"* On the stage, a big, happy poster catches my eye: FREE YOUR MIND AND YOUR ASS WILL FOLLOW, it says, expressing a fundamental gay idea that also has a lot in common with traditional Christian notions about the primacy of spirit over flesh. (I like the poster, but I keep wondering if it couldn't work the other way, as well.)

Though the P.A. system is still wailing *desire!*, the crowd hushes abruptly when Ephen Colter, a wan-looking young man in tiny dreadlocks, wilts his way to the mike. Colter, an American Studies grad student with a languorous air like a dying priest, has toddled to the lectern to breathe out the essentially religious purpose of tonight's event: "Tonight . . . we'll *address* . . . the increasing *hostility* . . . to public *sex* in the *culture.*"

Colter is wearing a skimpy tube top, but his voice is pious and not very desirous. There is a fusty, culture-defending tone to it, rather like, come to think of it, William Bennett, or maybe Allan Bloom, defending a sacred culture from barbarians. It seems more appropriate by the minute that the theme song for tonight's forum is dedicated to a deity from classical antiquity. Sex Panic! numbers more academicians among its members than any other gay protest group in history, which makes this event an even more interesting airing of the mind-body question than the sign about the best way to free a person's ass. Some of the most famous names in postmodern theory have prepared indecipherable treatises for this teach-in— so they can lecture us on the supremacy of the flesh, and plot sensation's victory over the mind.

Nonetheless, this evening promises some thrills. Behind me, a flock of gay, lesbian, and bisexual NYU undergraduates breathlessly point out the academic stars in attendance. "That's Michael Warner."

"Shit! He's young."

"That's his boyfriend in the blue shirt—in the second row."

"That's Allan Bérubé, talking to the dyke with the buzz cut."

"That's Ann Pellegrini. She works at Barnard." (Actually, she has moved up the ladder of theory even further— to Harvard.)

"That's Mo B. Dick, the gender illusionist." (Dick's not an academic, but she is a star, and this group likes stars because, as the song says, they "burn in a silver flame.")

"The gender what?"

"Or you might call her a drag king." One tall boy is the principal informant of the other students, and he uses his new terminology proudly. He proceeds to give his companions a long, earnest list of hanky codes, gay male sexual insignia that were used in the '70s and, unbeknownst to the undergrads, are barely used today. "Yellow is water sports. Brown is scat. Green is *ménage*."

"That's so cool."

Meanwhile, Colter welcomes us, after a fashion, vamping at the mike and meaningfully spreading his legs. "Thank you for coming. We're going to start in about three *months*." It's his proud joke about gay tardiness and unreliability.

Given this group's composition, it's not too surprising that its members want sex to debase them, to knock them down to earth. But try as they may to give themselves over to pure carnality and unthinking passion, they do not quite succeed. "With the closing of [the bar] Cake, white, Latino and black queers of the Lower East Side lost an important stage to rehearse their identities," rails NYU professor José Muñoz. Ann Pellegrini is even more feverishly agitated: "The sign LESBIAN is being deployed as a wedge against public sexuality."

But if you listen closely, you'll get the message. Sex is always "wicked," and therefore must always be defended, because the unethical, the aberrant, and the unspeakable are the things that liberate us. Pellegrini is angry at those who think "lesbian relationships preclude power imbalances based on one partner's gender," because, apparently, she likes power imbalances and does not want us to be accused of ever abstaining from them. "I'm not here calling for positive images. Frankly, they leave me cold." Like someone who can only be excited by unloyalty, she hates "this idea that lesbians are serially semper fi."

Most of these people seem to think that in order to support promiscuity, you need to detest monogamy the way that God hates the Prince of Darkness. For the same reason, the word *moral* is used at this forum only as a negative, and people reserve their greatest outrage for being accused of it. (Writer Lisa Duggan is highly offended to hear gay male sexual conservatives refer to "the greater moral superiority and domestic monogamy of lesbians." "That's exactly what you'd hear in a right-wing church!" she fumes. Well, not exactly.)

I understand why they're offended. It's rather infuriating to be assumed to be asexual, an assumption gay men like Larry Kramer and many other men like to make about lesbians. And when people assume you are "good" all your life, you get more than a tiny hankering to be evil, if only for half a moment, when they're watching. It's as though people thought that you'd never tasted of the tree of knowledge, never gotten to make the confounding choice. The strange thing is that Sex Panic! appears to accept traditional sexual morality on its face—apparently believing that "morality" is exactly what the right says it is.

Because the right has called sexually active people evil, Sex Panicers have decided evil's what they are. In effect, they never *have* made the choice.

"I want extortion, racketeering," "bisexual fag hag" artist Penny Arcade shrieks into the mike. "I want everything to come back."

Utopians speak approvingly of love, reciprocity, self-respect. Therefore, Sex Panicers take anything smacking of egalitarianism, self-protection, or concern for others as the devil's work.

Warm regard for oneself or for others is to be avoided. Sex is about danger, and opening to the dark. A skinny, very young male performance artist named Dan Bacalzo gets up and gives an emotionally naked monologue about his ambivalent desires around unsafe sex. Physically, he is nearly naked, too; looking at him, I feel a bit like his john. "To have a dick up my ass without a condom . . . I am scared that I will never know what that feels like. And I am scared that I will know what it feels like, and immediately regret it."

It's both moving and repelling to hear him. We all bend forward to look at him more closely and to enjoy every syllable of his confession; his voice is larded with shame, and misplaced trust in us. "I remember how it felt when I got fucked on stage at the safer sex event, and how I felt that night that I would have consented to anything." I love him for making himself so open like this, but I also want to throw a blanket over him, protect him from feeling like he *has* to be exposed on every level, vulnerable to whatever the sexual universe demands. "I remember how I felt when someone asked if I had ever been a top and I had to say no."

At a Sex Panic! event three months later at a comfortable lesbian bar on Houston Street, the Sex Panic! greeter, Juno Williamson, confides that she has gotten involved because "all the tawdriness of New York" has been cleaned up; she can no longer find the dirt and violence that she craves. Williamson, twenty-five, feels nostalgia for the days when "Broadway in the Village, even in the middle of the day, used to be a little scary." She's from New Jersey and used to take the train in on the weekends for the scariness.

Loy, a straight man who manages a swing band, tells me proudly about "the gay gangsters and their drag queen girlfriends" who regularly come to hear them play. He waits for me to say how impressed I am that homosexual Mafiosi know and like him. "Wow," I say.

"They really like swing, you know."

Then novelist Bruce Benderson gets up, in an absurd black velvet shirt with tassels like a bad fashion designer's idea of the afternoon tea-wear of the Marquis de Sade, to read a marvelously lyrical passage from his forthcoming novel about the changes in Times Square. It is an ode to everything he loves that is no more: "O'Neil's, which once served teenage hustlers and their working-class johns, several blocks from Cocktails, where the crack was hidden in the ceiling tiles and the Latin Kings came with their girls . . . the Minnesota Strip, which was Eighth Avenue between Forty-seventh Street and Forty-eighth, so called because so many runaways arriving from Minnesota used the strip for begging and hustling . . . the Times Square [bar, filled with] Latin Kings and hustlers who would invite their tricks to the pay-by-hour hotel next door . . ." He is a wonderful prosodist, but what he celebrates make me nauseous. The teenagers he loves to see renting themselves out to adults are starving, and homeless. Most of them are on the run from sexual abuse at home.

Benderson continues with his paean to the good old days. Many of these teenage runaways, he says, stayed off and on at Covenant House, a charity run by Father Bruce Ritter, who in time "was revealed as something less than a saint." The Sex Panic! audience may or may not know what this means—Ritter was revealed to have required sex from many of his young charges—but this is their response: "Go, Bruce!"

After one more expression of regret for the loss of the teen flesh trade, Benderson ends with this bitter coda: "It's gone. It's finished. It's over. Forget it." The romanticism of danger and ugliness in his piece is as great as any romanticism the religious right could make of marriage.

℣

And yet . . . There *are* wonderful things in the darkness. It's not for nothing that Benderson reads like Ginsberg and Verlaine. His catalog of beautiful malefactors comes straight from Whitman, who knew a thing or two about the relationship between God and evil. "This is the meal pleasantly set," Whitman wrote. "It is for the wicked just the same as the righteous. . . . I make appointments with all. . . . I will not have a single person slighted or left away. The keptwoman and sponger and thief are hereby invited . . . the venerealee is invited . . . What blurt is it about virtue and about vice? Evil propels me, and reform of evil propels me. . . . I stand indifferent, / My gait is no fault-finder's or rejecter's gait, / I moisten the roots of all that has grown." Christ invited tax gatherers and sinners to dine with him, and Whitman wants to do the same. His list of "bad people" is weak stuff by today's standards, focusing on the disreputable, not the destructive. But were he alive today perhaps he would say: The sexual abuser is invited. The batterer and murderer are hereby invited. The rapist is invited.

All of us have something in us like the desire to exploit starving boys, the desire to abuse little girls. The impulse to beat up prostitutes, menace wimps, degrade lovers, just because it feels so mysteriously satisfying to treat people like dirt. Do we get anywhere by not talking about it? No. But embracing it uncritically doesn't get us very far, either. Bowing down and adoring the worm within the soul, as Benderson does, is not the solution—is it?

I became a gay activist to get away from the violative monster within me. But it hasn't worked. Not gay liberation, not feminism, not even sexual liberation can ease that howling monster, or deliver it from me. I can neither soften it nor expel it. I can't quench that fire.

Sex and love are bound up with it, I don't know why; but they make us want to surrender ourselves to the monster, or sacrifice people to it.

Sex Panic! wants us to stop fighting the process. If morality didn't exist, why would unethical conduct trouble us? And if sex is always good, then it can never hurt us.

Moralists fear all of sex, because touching the Other makes them remember the monster. Sex Panic! fears none of sex, so it can pretend that no monster exists.

❧

As for me . . .

I remember a sex without monsters. When I went to a lesbian backroom bar in the early '90s, the kind Larry Kramer would hate and Ann Pellegrini would approve, as I remember it there was only exquisite touching, kind strangers, women putting their mouths around me. Soft flanks, New Wave music playing somewhere around us, and no fear . . . It was very much like the heavenly balloons onstage. Innocent pleasure. Candy.

There was nothing to hurt me there because, strictly speaking, there wasn't an other. Oh, there were other human beings there whom I respect to this day, but I didn't have to relate to them. "Two paradises 'twere in one," Marvell said, "to live in paradise alone."

3

Cross

There has to be a better way. But what is it? I can't imagine how to connect with the other without encountering the Afflicter. For a long time, I fought off Old Nick by fighting the religious right, an other who was explicitly and obviously my afflicter. By spending most of my time and energy fighting them, at least I knew I was fighting the monster.

They squeezed the joy out of life wherever they went—making sex illegal, censoring libraries, defunding battered-women's shelters. Defeating the ERA, supporting corporal punishment, actually backing death-squad dictatorships in Central America—the list went on and on. I couldn't think of a better group to identify with the Devil.

But there was always something uncanny about my hatred of them. There was something libidinal about it, actually. I adored having them to hate, with their weird intensity, their burning concern for the very same issues that kept me awake at night. Their sputtering accents, like brief flares in the somnolent sameness of America. Their bizarre love for "the babies." Their bad clothes. Their strong terror of people like me.

How could I not love to hate them? They were my opposite, but in personality much the same as me: driven, furious. Ravenous for *something*. And they put all that energy at the service of injustice. These people scared me so much it was exciting.

It's not surprising, then, that when the Promise Keepers come along, I get hot under the collar about them. I am frightened and titillated almost more than I can stand. Feminists call them the "kinder, gentler" face of sexism— a sort of Trojan horse of the Christian right, sent to invade our gates. They claim to be our best friends. I decide to do to them what they do to unsuspecting women.

🍂

I walk into the arena more slowly and grandly than I have ever walked into anything in my life. Inside, I am shaking. There are men all around me, crowding so close I can count their nose hairs, smell their sweat. *Men* are *different from women,* I think, surprised. That's something I have never wanted to believe. But today, I am trying to be one.

I've put on a mustache and bound my breasts to get inside the Promise Keepers, the Christian right group that makes men see God. Feeling their muscles through dirty T-shirts as we pack too closely, smelling their incredible variety of stale and unwelcoming scents, I want to see these grunts see God; but what I'm doing feels like a scary violation of them, as though I were entering not just their sacred, men-only space, but their bodies, themselves. As we jam inside the St. Petersburg Thunderdome, it is their alienness I feel, not the kinship I have always felt with men. They are Southerners in baseball caps, truck-driver men, little boys shrieking for attention, teenagers smirking and punching each other in the upper arm; men I would steer clear of in bars or even highway rest stops, men who go to strip clubs and stick dollars in the women's panties; men with that sad scrunch to their faces that comes from never expressing anything except maybe fervor for the Broncos. Some of their alienness is class and some's geography, but the really basic difference is, they're guys. My men friends back home, even the straight ones, are less *male* than these men. All of the men I care about quote poetry and talk easily about weeping. *These* men in their Christian versions of the Gold's Gym T-shirt (CROSS TRAINING with a logo of the cross imagined as a dumbbell), in their big windbreakers and their endless silence with each other, are a different species.

I feel bad about penetrating their time alone together. I pitch my legs ridiculously wide the way they do, aping their walk as I approach the outer door. But maleness remains a mystery to me, and its burdens and pains are basically beyond me, unshareable. I'm pretty butch, but I can't really know what it is like to grow up as a man, no matter how many girlfriends like my big black boots or how much the thought of wearing dresses bothers me. I feel like Pentheus, the Theban king who dressed as a woman and pranced around so that he could spy on the Maenads' sacred rites together. He wanted to ogle and leer, to see what women do when they get together at religious orgies men can't come to. *What do two women do together?* The Maenads tore him into little pieces.

There are fifty thousand Christian men in here, and me; the Promise Keepers press office didn't return my calls for two months, so here I am, in my usual cheeky way, muscling in where I've been barred. PK does allow women reporters into its events, but they apparently weren't too keen on having one like me, some radical lesbo from *Ms.* In time-honored lesbian-feminist fashion, I've come without an invitation. It's a bit of derring-do, like the lesbians in Britain who swung from the rafters of Parliament to protest an anti-gay vote. "Crash the party," as ACT UP would say—enter where you're not wanted, and shake things up! The disguise makes the whole escapade even more exciting, a testament to my bravery and hardiness—my butchness, in a word. Or, to be even more real about it, my balls. When you get right down to it, I make a very good man. "If you were male," I hear my old friend Polly telling me, "you'd be completely insufferable."

Despite my qualms, I feel more than entitled. The Promise Keepers have committed an even worse sin than denying me a press pass—they believe in patriarchy! As I swagger around looking for a seat, I recall the words that preacher Tony Evans wrote in his contribution to *Seven Promises of a Promise Keeper,* the first of four inspirational Promise Keepers best-sellers. "The first thing you do is sit down with your wife and say something like this: 'Honey, I've made a terrible mistake. I've given you my role. I gave up leading this family, and I forced you to take my place. Now I must reclaim that role.' Don't misunderstand what I'm saying here. I'm not suggesting that you *ask* for your role back, I'm urging you to *take it back*. . . . Be sensitive. Listen. Treat the lady gently and lovingly. But *lead!*" I have to clamp down on my facial muscles to keep from smirking; in another context, most of the lesbians I know would find this sexy. It's a fantasy that could have come straight out of *The Persistent Desire*, the popular butch-femme anthology lesbians have been keeping for years in their bedside tables.

But these guys mean it for real, the irritated politico in me insists on rasping. So they do. In his essay, Evans, an African American who is the pastor for the Dallas Mavericks basketball team, has an even more frightening suggestion for "you ladies who might be reading this": *"Give it back!"* With his essay in mind, I've dressed flamboyantly patriarchal, not just boyish. The sixteen-year-old Christian boy I am depicting wears a glow-in-the-dark Mike Tyson T-shirt and a backwards baseball cap with the logo of a comic-book character called The Punisher.

Lesbians detest this side of men—but we also love it. When the singer Phranc did a national concert tour in which she impersonated Neil Diamond, her lesbian audience grooved to the male obnoxiousness she brought so fulsomely to the role, crooning out a hit parade of repellently sexist tunes from "If I Were a Carpenter" to "Lay, Lady, Lay." She swaggered as she sang Neil's lyrics about wantin' his woman to be "walkin' behind me." Then the crowd tossed her their panties.

Lesbians are haunted by this gross, imperious man—and they're hardly the only ones. Strutting around the bleachers in my punk goatee, I know that my obsession with male domination is like almost everyone's in this society—not just erotic, but extending into every aspect of everyday life. When I have an argument with someone at the grocer's, I worry about who screwed who, who was the female in our interaction. When I take a Killer Fitness class at the gym, I think about who in the class makes me look like shit with their muscles and conditioning, and who I beat like the wispy things they are. Male domination pervades my life, but it pervades men's lives even more. They are its standard-bearers, the ones who are painfully tested every day to make sure they're (still) real men. Women are not so tested; the cycle of perpetual challenge and contempt men are subjected to spills over into my life occasionally, but it *is* their life.

I'm afraid of being beaten up or worse, here, for exactly that reason. Men care about these painful contests even more than I do and do not like them to be mocked. "This is the first time the Thunderdome has been full to capacity!" a PK organizer is yelling at us as I sit down, his image made gigantic on a video screen. "I can see Jesus dribbling down the court right now. You can take Michael Jordan, but I'll take Jesus! *Nothin' but net!*" The men roar. The logo for this year's Promise Keepers national tour, "Raise the Standard," is everywhere: on men's chests, on their caps, on a giant banner hanging from the ceiling. The image is disconcerting: three outrageously muscular men's arms (white, black, and brown) hoist a huge flagpole at an angle that makes it look exactly like an erection. Their fists grip the pole; the flag, which dwarfs the sun and everything else on the banner, bears a kingly crown on which is written PK.

The Promise Keepers seem to like picking phallic names for their national events. The '97 Washington rally with five hundred thousand men was called "Stand in the Gap," and many local chapters sold their men promotional T-shirts with a distendedly turgid Washington Monument. In this Florida basketball stadium, guys all around me have insufferably masculine slogans on *their* T-shirts, too: A MAN'S MAN IS A GODLY MAN. AS IRON SHARPENS IRON, ONE MAN SHARPENS ANOTHER. MIGHTY SON OF GOD. But as I meet my rowmates, I find myself starting to relax. Jose, on my right, is about thirty-five, sweaty, taciturn, and kind, with a little paunch. Charlie, on my left, is from the suburbs, rueful and muscular in a polo shirt; I like them. They are young married men, repressed, but with a barely detectable air of longing—sexual? parental? for friends? They pass me pictures of their very small children. I like their eyes, which are sadder and much more open than the eyes I've usually seen in ballparks.

I can tell that they like me, too, or at least my sixteen-year-old-boy other self. Tenderness is stopped up in Charlie and Jose somewhere; looking at me somehow lets it out. "You came here all the way from New York all by yourself?!" Charlie marvels at me. "I never could have done it at your age." They clap me on the back; I feel an approbation I have never felt before. It's weird how good this feels. I ask Charlie if he'd like a soda from the refreshment stand and he looks surprised and even touched. I fleetingly remember that most men above the age of ten are afraid to be too nice to other men; *giving* as much as a Coke has implications that ought to be avoided in all circumstances.

But perhaps men would like to become less afraid. As the Maranatha! Men's Promise Band starts singing "Abba Father," one of the gushiest hymns in the evangelical songbook, I look around at fifty thousand men stammeringly trying to find a way to tell their Father God they love Him. "*Oh, Abba, Father . . .*" It is strange hearing men's voices sound this soft. Jose sings with his eyes tightly shut. My other rowmate grips my hand and doesn't let it go. They look, suddenly, different from the men I've seen shouting incomprehensibly at Knicks games, or swinging police nightsticks, or smacking their lips at me in the street: the really masculine men in my town.

"Some people find that the same problems follow them from relationship to relationship," says a sandy-haired man at the podium. The men around me listen intently. "New relationship, and you're doing the same old stuff." Well, this is a new thing for conservative men to be preaching about—or any men, really. But all these guys are looking at him with an air of recognition.

"Many times we want to say the problem is in the White House, or the Senate, or the state house. But God says, the problem is with my people! I'm telling you the problem is with *us!*" I'm starting to react as though my soda had spoken to me. When was the last time I heard a right-wing group—or even a *left-wing* group—say this? "When we find the same problems in a different relationship, it's because we're running from our problems! We're running from our conscience." Jesus. Greg Laurie, a well-known Christian author, is speaking directly out of my head, saying things I know are true *about me*—that at the moment are some of the truest things about me. I never expected to hear a religious-right person say anything so real, but that's not the most surprising thing about the voice entering my skull. I am in the presence of something holy; everything this speaker says is so important for me to hear that, although I don't believe in God in this sense, it feels like God is talking to me. "Nineveh was a city famous for its cruelty." I've been realizing lately how cruel I've been to the people in my family. How insanely tyrannical with my friends. "They tortured people there." *Ungiving* has often been my middle name. "We need to become loving fathers and husbands." If I think men are ungiving, I ought to look at me, grudging of everything, locked up tighter than a miser's safe under thick bars. "Jonah, he was the original chicken of the sea." Me too, refusing to give love so that I won't be taken over; it all comes from fear.

Men stretch out their palms to Laurie in the gospel signal, a curiously feminine gesture. They are waving at him from their seats and even giving him the "disco point" to show the man he's right; he has excited *them,* too. On the video screen, a man gazes at the camera sadly and reports: "My main problem in life is dealing with relationships." It's very moving, and not just because men don't usually say this sort of thing. It's been my problem, too, although I'm not a man. I could be the manliest of manlies, if this is how masculinity is judged. My barriers are immense; my strength is hollow. I have to ceaselessly think about the prestige and power I command, or I am nothing. I even have to think about my money! Even my fucking money; every day, buying an expensive lunch, I feel *real,* finally demonstrably superior. Buying my lovers dinner, I feel all-powerful. I feel like a sixty-year-old CEO with a twenty-year-old babe on his knee. Why do I need this?

"*I'm* not as important as I used to be," the man from the video says. "What's important to me now is my relationship with my wife, my relationship with my family." All my life, I've felt entitled to hurt people. I've used my politics as an excuse to be vicious; I've used my experiences of oppression, personal and political, as tokens entitling me to take thousands of free punches at friends, semi-friends, adversaries, and people who just happened to be handy. I've enjoyed writing bad reviews; I've found it intoxicating to be hurtful in print. Lesbian, straight, or gay, white, beige, or brown, everyone has borne my blows. And in my mind, everyone has deserved them. I don't need to be moral; I only need to be strong. That's been my credo.

"The point is, God gives second chances! Listen, men, we need to turn from our wicked ways!" Laurie cuts in. "We need to repent all our known sins." I look up. "God says, no heart is so heavy that I cannot bear."

I swear I'm not a Christian. But the words are holy; they lighten me. I've always wanted to be saved. I chuckle to myself. It is hilarious, finding some grace at the Promise Keepers. I always knew my job would get me places. "But you must do it *now!*" Laurie bleats. "The Bible says, *Today* is the day of salvation!" Oh, it's the altar call. The band starts playing the music they play on game shows just before you lose your turn. "In a moment, it'll be too late!" We're supposed to walk down onto the basketball court in the next three minutes if we want to accept God's grace. They have "prayer volunteers" standing by to help us. "It's almost time!" My epiphany is turning into a Buy Now Or See the Price Go Up promotion. Finally—what the hell!—I sprint down onto the field. I'm practically the last one. A middle-aged Hispanic man agrees to be my prayer volunteer; he's already pastoring to a twenty-year-old guy, but he puts his hand on me, too. And we pray together. It's unbelievably sweaty, and time seems to stop. I'm glad I'm here. It's not that I think this moment has saved me, exactly, but I want to dedicate this moment to the changes I've been making in my life, of which I want to make many more. "Lord, we pray for the soul of Jim and of this brother," says the prayer-guy. "Don," I whisper. "Don." At the end, we all three hug so tightly I'm afraid they might be able to tell I have breasts. It's a much soggier, smellier embrace than I usually think of as characterizing religious experiences, but I want to acknowledge the mercy I am feeling, the sweet mercy I've been shown. On the way back up to my seat, I get a little packet with the Gospel of John and a form to fill out ("The following statement best describes the action I am taking. Check one: 1. *Acceptance.* I just personally accepted Jesus Christ as my Lord and Savior . . .") Truthfully, I detest the Gospel of John, but that's not important. What's more important is, I'm acknowledging an opening in my life.

When I say I've been shown mercy, I don't mean by God, but by people—which is even more beautiful. Mercy is such a staggering concept. I have a chance to tell everyone I love that I love them! And to know that they love me, too! I don't have to be a despot! I can be a friend! I can be a family member!

Into this bath of red-hot love slides T. D. Jakes, the next speaker. He's a guy with a charming, fat face and a black beard like a bull's, a black minister from West Virginia whose books, like Laurie's, do enormously well on the evangelical circuit. Jakes's voice goes far, far down the basso register, so that it seems to be coming out of the ground, deeper than any other Promise Keeper's—like God's voice in a De Mille movie. And he says: "Let's read Acts 3:1–8! Peter and John were on their way up to the temple! Now a man who was lame from his mother's womb used to be carried there, and laid every day by the gate of the temple called Beautiful Gate, to beg from the people as they went in. He was lame! We're talking about a man who had a problem *in one area*. He had a weakness *in one area of his life*."

He whispers fiercely: "*Every man in this room has somewhere in his life an area of challenge!* And sometimes it's so personal, we don't want anyone to know it." Even mentioning that you have a problem makes you less of a man, other Promise Keepers note; officially, men aren't supposed to have problems. As Randy Phillips, the president of Promise Keepers, says: "We're afraid of being overwhelmed. We're afraid of being killed. We're afraid of being annihilated. We're afraid of being violated." And admitting problems means that all of these are possible: we can be hurt no matter how male we are. Well, according to myself, *I'm* not supposed to have problems, either. Having problems or pain in any measure makes me less than the omnipotent human being I believe I am supposed to be. But T. D. Jakes says softly: "Somewhere in your life, there is an *it* that must be faced and reckoned with, and until you deal with it you will be hindered in your life. . . . This man was by the gate called Beautiful! He was in a beautiful place, but he had an ugly problem! Have you ever been in a beautiful place but had an ugly problem?"

All the time. Just all the time. But now Jakes says something even more exciting than that: "I refuse to walk past a brother's pain. I'm going to reach out and touch his life, even if it takes all night." He recounts how, in the story, Peter tells the lame man, "I have no silver or gold, but what I have I give you: in the name of Jesus Christ of Nazareth, walk." Then "he grasped him by the right hand and pulled him up; and at once his feet and ankles grew strong; he sprang up, stood on his feet, and started to walk." As social philosophy, this is pretty repellent stuff; I would not want to make common cause with anyone who applied this idea to economics (or even to miracle-less physical disability). But on the level of *psychic* disability it is pretty true. "You have to decide how to deal with the areas of conflict in you," Jakes rumbles. "We can go to war! We can fight with nations! We can beat our chest and brag about our own strength and power and fight! But the greatest enemy that I ever had to fight is the enemy in me."

Me too. Me too, me too, me too.

"We cannot leave this room walking over wounded men. But we must give the man a hand. Touch somebody and say, Give the man a hand!" We all touch each other. "There's something about men touching men that's miraculous," Jakes says. "'When they took him by the hand, *immediately* his ankles received strength.' It was immediate! That's the power of men touching other men!" Well! All over the stadium, men have been doing just that. There are groups of three, four, and five men caressing one another to Jakes's words. In the seats in front of me are two young men I like to think of as a couple; they started out only rapping each other in the arm affectionately, but their arms have been around each other's waists for half an hour. Charlie and Jose and I have been holding hands. On the other side of the stadium, radiant, swishy men wave giant Promise Keepers flags. The men here don't *all* look like truck drivers, I finally notice; some look like Radical Faeries, with long Jesus hair and love beads. I wouldn't be surprised to see a few of them blowing multicolor bubbles or handing out daisies to the rest of us. Others have gym bodies and are wearing the tight clothes to show them off. My older rowmates don't want to stop holding my hands. The couple in front of me continues to hold each other all the way to the refreshment stand and the bathroom.

"You must decide, this is a turning point for me! *In the name of Jesus Christ, walk!*" And they say *we're* proselytizers. "That is the name that will liberate you from the jail you have been held in!" I love the poetry this man speaks in. "That is going to be the name that delivers the violent man. That is going to be the name that delivers the man that hurts his children. That is going to be the name that delivers the drug addict and the homosexual."

A brief moment of cognitive dissonance, as though a fly were distracting me from something holy. It's horrible that he thinks becoming moral means you have to cease to be homosexual. But does it make the rest of his speech less beautiful? No.

꿈

I'm feeling so much love that I feel like the bridegroom in the Song of Songs. *There's so much here,* I write in my schoolboy's notebook, *all piled up for me.* I feel a wonder and magic I have certainly never felt while with a right-wing group before. Loving the Promise Keepers even though they're in the religious right feels pretty special. It gives me something. Some sense of moral paradox—if there is good in *them,* who believe homosexuality is wrong and give money to the clinic blockaders, then there is liable to be good in the most monstrously evil persons I will ever meet, and mercy will always be required of me.

I believe that something in me has been permanently made right. It didn't happen just from my coming here, but coming here's been part of it, and I am grateful. I feel clothed in light. Maybe I ought to start a lesbian branch of the Promise Keepers. Maybe I will become reconciled to everyone I have ever hated. Maybe I ought to preserve my Mike Tyson T-shirt as a memento of a holy weekend in my life.

The next day, my mustache starts to melt. It has been applied one hair at a time with spirit gum, and it's vanishing rapidly in the heat. I'm afraid to look at the men, again. They note my wariness and start looking suspiciously at *me.* I dash home and reapply it, but it's not the same. Sunday is worse than Saturday. Perhaps I'm less ecstatic because it begins with a speaker asking us to clap for the grandfathers in the audience, then the fathers, then the sons. I don't think men deserve applause just for siring children—or just for *being* male children, either. Seems to me they get enough applause for that already. Well, maybe I'm just jealous because no one's clapping for me.

But there are some more beautiful things even today, the day I fail to keep my promise to sit with Charlie and Jose because I am queasy about getting even closer with them. Joseph Garlington, a minister from Pittsburgh, lets us know that "Jesus didn't say, 'Blessed are the macho'! He didn't say, 'Blessed are those that have it together'!" I love this. We're always told we have to have it together or we're shit. But then he says some things that sound more like the disturbing right wing I am used to. Garlington, who once participated in an authoritarian church movement known as "shepherding," tells us that "God created us with an innate desire to see someone or something as superior to ourselves. We were created to worship. It's like God programmed you to be a worshipper." It turns out that his anti-macho preachings stem from a belief that men must humiliate themselves before God. His problem with macho men is that they just don't deprecate themselves enough.

At Garlington's behest, we all sing *"I desire to worship and obey."* Then Garlington bids us to abase ourselves "in whatever way the spirit moves you." Some kneel, some bow, some prostrate themselves fully—a favorite posture of the Promise Keepers, it turns out. It's very weird. Men around me start to moan about their sins. "I am not worthy . . ." "Oh, God! Have mercy, Father God! Have mercy . . ." "Oh, God. I give you my love. I give you my life.

Helpless. Yes, Lord, closer to you." Why do they think love and morality have anything to do with humiliation? Why do they believe God wants them to lick His boots?

Later I remember a weird fact about men: They *like* to abase themselves. I keep mistakenly telling people this conference took place in *St. Augustine,* Florida, not St. Petersburg. It's just that all this weeping, mortification, red faces, sorrowful confessions, and paroxysms of hangdog shame are a part of a historical male trajectory that dates back at least as far as that most male and ecstatically hangdog of saints, Augustine. *Honey, I have sinned!* As we usually conceive of it, repentance is male, not female. Women aren't supposed to sin to begin with, but men are expected to do things for which they'll have to say they're sorry later.

No wonder the Promise Keepers seem to enjoy addressing God as though he were their dominatrix. For one thing, it makes it okay to have been *bad.* For another, it is a great relief to bow at last before the Phallic Mother or some better man than you. Affirming your worthlessness before God and women *is a release,* if you're a man. It means you can stop worrying about who is on top. You can stop worrying about whether you're even half the man you are supposed to be. "Father, we *yield* ourselves to you," I'll hear a twenty-five-year-old Promise Keeper pray on the Washington Mall two years later, "to *receive* your forgiveness and grace and to *feel* your righteousness." All the verbs sound so female, or at least what men imagine as female. It is a wish-fulfillment, pure and simple.

We sing, *"Now my heart's desire is to know You more / to be found in You / to be known as Yours."* This is not male domination, but it is hardly feminism, either. If it resembles anything in my life, it would be the period when I wanted to be the creature of Dionysus, or Aphrodite. Self-abasement is required for anyone who wants to be taken over by a god. I imagine these men in little French-maid's uniforms, clutching feather dusters instead of Bibles. Charlie, writhing on the cement floor near me, would enjoy it just the same.

Is my confession just as fantasy-laden as theirs? Am I exclaiming how wicked I've been so that someone will kiss me and make me better?

After my article on the Promise Keepers conference appears, I get a phone call from a very nice man who lives in Nashville. He's a Promise Keeper who liked my article: how wonderful. And in any case, he is thoroughly engaging: "I like radicals," he growls into the phone, "because I am a passionate person!" Rick Brautigan, thirty-eight, is a sports editor at a major Southern daily. (Imagine that, my secretly bigoted inner self says. He is an evangelical, but he can read and do sports coverage, too.)

His letters are flattering: "I was greatly impressed by you in our first chat on the phone. You strike me as not only a bright and thoughtful woman, but caring and compassionate as well. I sense a sincerity in you that is rare and refreshing." Later: "I thoroughly enjoy being able to speak with you." His letters are Jane Austen, but his phone-talk is James Dean. Rick doesn't want me to think all evangelicals hate gay people and feminists: "I get so *angry* at those Christians who are judgmental! You're the daughter of the King!"

On the phone, we have long conversations about our synergies. I am delighted at the prospect of becoming friends with him—a real friendship with a real conservative evangelical! What a sign that I have reached out, gotten beyond the superficial, and had a real conversation with the Other! I pat myself on the back for being able to go beyond the limits of my ideology. It is like holding Charlie and Jose, but it is realer, and it goes on for much longer.

He sends me an exquisitely beautiful coffee-table book on the Olympics that he has co-authored. It is inscribed: "To Donna, a special, sensitive woman with a remarkable writing talent from our Lord." Don't think I am immune to flattery about my writing—from evangelicals or anybody else. And don't think I am immune to beautiful presents, either. I may be feeling "holy" as I come to believe that the religious right is not made up of monsters, but a lot of this is just the desire to love. It feels good to love people, whether they are monstrous or not. And it feels good to be loved, and to get presents.

In every conversation Rick mentions the Lord and how I really ought to get closer to Him, but I tune it out. "I terribly regret missing your annual preaching," I write when the coffee-table book comes. There is a romance-novel quality to our interaction; it is especially rousing to befriend someone from the enemy camp, as though Brautigan were a good-looking spy for the forces that wanted to seize my grandma's castle. And it is especially alluring to be like Christ with him—and meet him only with love.

Rick writes that some lesbian friends of his are coming to hear him preach, "with their precious daughter." I am melted, reading this. He really does love us! They are even coming home with him afterward for dinner with his family. It is a mythic reconciliation narrative, kind of like the "Homecoming" TV-movie episode of the Waltons. "I know this is probably totally out the question," he writes, like the gentleman he is, "but I thought I'd at least let you know in the remote chance you could join us." Waves of oozy good fellowship curl up from the paper and into my ready heart. The lesbo family at the dinner table really sets my bells ringing. I'm going to get *really* schmaltzy any minute now and start declaiming Jesus' parable of the prodigal son. That parable is about me, in part. I have a strong, strong desire to be embraced by those I've hated, even those I've hated for good reason. And I have almost as burning a desire to be embraced by those who've hated *me*.

Thankfully, I don't have to declaim the story of the prodigal, because a Promise Keeper chivalrously steps in to do it for me. Back on the stage in St. Petersburg, Greg Laurie relates how, after the bad son had left home and lost all his money, he comes back to his rich family at last. "His father comes running up to him. And the son thinks, *he can't wait to get his hands around my neck!* But his father runs up to him, throws his arms around him, and welcomes him, and kisses him over and over again!"

That's sort of how I'm feeling when Rick writes, "Thank you for your patience and gentle spirit." There's a vision in me of a world where the lamb really *can* lay down with the lion, and I think maybe this is what is happening when Rick and I say nice things to each other. I want to lay down with the lion, more than anything; and I'd like to pardon the lion. Most of us *are* the lion sometimes, anyhow; if we want to pardon ourselves, we have to pardon him. But it's so fucking hard! Yet Brautigan makes me think that the lion-lamb kiss of peace is possible. He says, "There is no way I believe I am more caring than you are." He even dares to make fun of other fundies to me: In the past, he writes, "All I could make of Christians was that they were small-minded, mean-spirited, judgmental hypocrites who knew nothing of good music and less about clothes."

After many nice talks in the course of a very pleasant year, we arrange a phone date for a long conversation. I want to take a leap and ask him what he thinks about homosexuality. He's never said and, amazingly, I have never asked. He's told me he liked gays, and I have been content with that. But something is making me want to go beyond the dumb bliss of our connection and into something more awkward and less pleasurable. This time I want to listen to the lion, not just bask in the warmth of his love.

He takes a long time in answering me. First he tells me, laboriously, the story of how he was saved—his long history of tolerance, gentle parents, "good career." It's not very clear what he needed to be saved *from*. Even then, incidentally, he was a fan of black sheep: friendly with "lesbian separatists" on campus, he claims, and his girlfriend was the state president for Pennsylvania NOW.

At the age of thirty, however, he had a "little crisis" of meaning. "I thought, 'Either accept the Bible, or throw it out.'" Rifling through the Bible to see whether it was trash or gold, "I was really blown away to see that Jesus didn't compromise." Rick was tremendously excited by the idea of not compromising, of not being allowed to compromise. "Men, in particular, really *compromise,* Donna. The truth is, men are born liars, they have no integrity, they don't keep their word. Yes, I really think men are more like that than women, Donna. We're born in sin."

"Do you really think men are intrinsically contemptible?"

"Donna, Rick may be a great guy, and he'll buy anybody a drink, but he's contemptible! Paul, in Romans, says, 'What a wretch am I!' 'Amazing Grace' says to save a wretch like me. My problem, Donna, was that I never felt enough like a wretch. But I know in my heart that I am closer to Adolf Hitler than I am to Jesus Christ."

Part of me loves this. Very few of my political buddies are willing to talk about how close they are to Hitler in their hearts. But part of me hates this "wretch"-talk worse than any other doctrine of the religious right. It is when people really think they're wretches that they *act* like Hitler. There is a difference, actually, between seeing the Hitler in you and identifying yourself as utterly unsalvageable, except by God's undeserved mercy. Just because there is a monster in the self doesn't mean that there isn't heroism and beauty there as well.

But Rick can only see the beast inside. "It's because of Adam. It's almost like genetics, you can't have two people who are spiritually dead, create a child who is spiritually alive. Christ was the first man since Adam who wasn't spiritually dead. And the only way anyone else can be, is to be on your knees to Him!"

"And yes," he says to me, almost whispering, "*this is offensive!* It's offensive to think that we have to bow to someone else to be saved. But as a theologian once said, this cause is offense!" I think I'm finally beginning to get him. Rick, like me, likes to give offense, and gives it regularly. "Before I was a Christian, I thought that you didn't ever *want* to be offensive. I was wrong! When I'm in a group of my buddies—unsaved buddies—and they're asking each other 'Who you running around with,' you know, little winking things, I say, 'It's wrong to treat your wife that way!'" When a colleague of his recently asked, "Who knows someone who can get this ticket fixed?" Rick spoke right up. "Do the right thing," he said. "Pay the damn ticket."

"It got under his skin," Rick says happily, "and he didn't like it."

In a way, this is totally appealing. In another way, it makes it sound torturous to be his friend.

More and more wretch-talk. "I have a problem with twelve-step groups," Rick says. "There's only one step that's right, and that's me on my knees. I am a slave to Jesus." But his very slavery is obnoxious and hard to bear. For the past forty minutes, he's been talking at me, not letting me get a word in edgewise, nagging me to convert every two seconds. It is exhausting, especially when he tells me that anger is a sin and that *he* has been freed from feeling it.

Finally, it is time to press my question again. I cannot believe I have never pushed him on this before: "What do you think about homosexuality?"

He really doesn't want to tell me. But he fudges: "Understand, when we talk about sin, we sin throughout the day. We sin by acts of commission and acts of omission. Paul says we sin when we are without faith."

But does he think homosexuality is a sin?

"If I'm an alcoholic, and I struggle with it, I'm still loved by God. But I can't fall to my knees and say, 'God, I love you, but this is the way I am and you can't change that.' In our new relationship with God, we shouldn't identify ourselves by our sin."

I should have known. Yet it's terribly surprising and disappointing. What was I expecting, loaves and fishes? I just go on asking questions like a reporter. "You're taking this from Paul."

"Right. Corinthians."

"Are you aware that there's a controversy about the Greek word he used? *Arsenokoitai* gets translated as 'homosexuals,' but scholars think it means specifically 'male prostitutes.'"

"We're playing legalisms here," he says brightly. "But the church is in support of womanhood, in support of the family, in support that we would love each other, do things as a *team*. It's clear to me that the model for that is the old-fashioned set-up between a man and a woman. Biologically, can't you see the kind of relationships you have is not what was intended?"

"I think I need to go," I say after a long while. But "No, don't go!" he pleads. "I know this is a struggle. But I can't compromise what I see here." It's very difficult to hang up on him. He's like a sort of taffy or molasses. Either that, or I am. Enraged as I am, it's hard to cut the connection. Finally, he coaxes, "Donna, I've dated lesbian women! I've been to gay bars—I'm utterly heterosexual, but I've been very opened. I went to the Copa in Fort Lauderdale, it was a fun, lively atmosphere—I was never tempted—but I couldn't reject those people. And I could never say that I'm more a child of God than you are. But I know how God wants women to be treated—I know the respect and honor and admiration and support that God wants you to have. And God is very offended that you don't have that."

In the end, he asks me about my relationship with my father and my earliest lesbian sexual fantasies before I tell him I don't want to talk anymore.

Does this make my being saved at the Promise Keepers all a farce? Does this make my desire to know them ridiculous, and my wish to give mercy insane?

In Washington, two years later, I try to figure it out. It's eight A.M and I am on the street in front of my hotel, watching little groups of Promise Keepers, five and six abreast, walk with purpose to the Capitol. With their stone-blank faces and their oversized male bodies, I can see why women fear them. We have little experience of groups of men that aren't menacing.

Women say that the fact that the Promise Keepers are a male group is ipso facto a reason they're a threat. "To date, every right-wing movement has been run by men," points out Al Ross, a progressive religious-right researcher who is a prime opponent of the group. But he himself is a man, and *his* organization, the Center for Democracy Studies, has been run by men as well. Does he doubt his own capacity to be moral?

The idea that men are naturally brutish (whether singly or in groups) did not originate with feminists. *Men Behaving Badly* works as the name of a TV show because this culture as a whole loves to assume that men are bad—this, in fact, could be called the bedrock sexist assumption. If men are naturally bad, we can't expect anything better from them.

But if men aren't naturally bad, doesn't there need to be some sort of men's movement helping them to change? Why should we expect them to do it all on their own, when women weren't able to change *their* behavior without a powerful social movement to support them?

In fact, the very reason men in groups so often do "bad" things is to reassure everyone that they're not getting together for some sissy purpose, like loving one another. Or even worse, trying to become better human beings. What would happen if men ever came together in the thousands for that reason?

I don't know, but it might look something like a Promise Keepers rally.

Yet people are afraid to hope, and in a way I cannot blame them. "They're the scariest thing I've ever seen," one woman tells another on Connecticut Avenue, as solemn-looking Promise Keepers shuffle by. These guys do look pretty stifled and shut down—much less melted and beautiful than the Promise Keepers I saw in St. Petersburg.

But maybe it's because they're in a strange city, with lots of manly men they don't know, being stared at by everyone. Like groups of second-graders, they plod self-consciously toward the Mall.

As we get near the grass, the feeling starts to change. There is a sense of at-home-ness as we all join up with one another, as though we were gay marchers and had finally found our rally. But there's something else that there's not much of at a gay and lesbian march (or at a Knicks game, either): a radical politeness. Men bump into each other and apologize profusely. When an eight-year-old boy, frustrated, starts to push his way through the crowd, his father crouches down and gently says, "You have to say, 'Excuse me, please.'" Several men walk by in T-shirts that read TODAY HE FORGIVES. Although I'm visibly a woman today, no one seems to think it odd that I'm here. A teenage boy cheerfully hands me a special-edition Promise Keepers Bible from a stack he is handing out: "You have a good day, ma'am."

A distinctly un–Christian Coalition T-shirt, on a tall black man: FINALLY, A DIET THAT ACTUALLY GUARANTEES WEIGHT LOSS above a photo of a man reaching into a garbage can. SUPPORT THE LOS ANGELES MISSION FOR THE HOMELESS, says the other side.

On the side of radical *im*politeness, there are the usual "in-your-face" Christian T-shirts that I've seen everywhere from Operation Rescue to so-called "radical Christian youth rallies." I have to say I feel a certain affection for these T-shirts, though they're annoying as all get-out. COMMIT OR LIVE IN THE PIT. SATAN IS AS UGLY AS SIN, 'CAUSE JESUS BEAT HIM WITH A STICK! CAN'T TAKE THE HEAT? GET

OUT OF HELL. They're hostile and asinine, but no more so than those Queer Nation–inspired stickers that say STRAIGHT IS STUPID or the button I have at home that reads LOSE YOUR HETEROSEXUALITY NOW—ASK ME HOW. Being countercultural is always horrid and magnificent at once. Meanwhile, a blond twenty-year-old is wearing one of these that I like: THE LORD WILL GO WITH YOU WHEREVER YOU GO. BE STRONG AND OUTRAGEOUS.

JESUS: DEFINING THE LINE THROUGH CHRISTIAN METAL says another. Near the Washington Monument, I find I'm standing in front of an enormous abortion banner with a picture of a fetus that looks like red jelly goo. Two thirteen-year-old boys are self-importantly holding the banner poles. Back in Florida, the Promise Keepers didn't mention abortion at all; here they will mention it twice from the stage, calling it "the worst form of child abuse" and showing a video where a man apologizes for "allowing" his wife to do it. A few paces away, a gaggle of Messianic Jews belt out what sound like Hasidic melodies as hundreds of Christian Promise Keepers listen, spellbound. "What is this?" someone whispers. "Oh, it's the *Jews!*" Messianic Jews are Jews for Jesus, and the Promise Keepers seem to feel it is a feather in their multicultural cap to have the Yids praise Christ here in their yarmulkas and *tallesim.* As the Jews make merry, dozens of uncircumcised men in bright pink shirts from the Sacred Assembly of Promise Keepers of Central Mississippi sway and clap to the *yiddische* beat.

"This is very both/and," I write in my notebook. So it is—perhaps the most "both/and" event I've ever been to.

Several hundred women, in denim, gingham, and motor-cycle leathers have turned out to support their husbands and friends, along with two hefty middle-aged women in Boy Scout uniforms. They are Troop Committee Leaders, but they've left their troops back home, and have just come here to root for the Promise Keepers. The only other woman I've ever seen in a Boy Scout uniform is my ex-girlfriend, the genderfuck king. The Promise Keepers do get around, I think as I see a youth-group-type Christian boy in a glowing green dog collar and studded leather armbands surrounded by his friends in T-shirts with a cross that says HIS PAIN, OUR GAIN. Next to him is a Christian motorcyclist wearing chains and whips at his belt.

Near the Capitol, many of us pop into the Air and Space Museum for the air-conditioning. But the Promise Keepers stay to ogle the Trident submarines. Men are swarming all around the model of the Tomahawk cruise missile, and I hear Promise Keepers in conversations like these: "It's air-craft-to-aircraft. *And* surface-to-air." "In Desert Storm, they could see it as it went through buildings." Fathers show their little boys their favorite smart bombs. Even bowing to Jesus doesn't save you from desires like this.

Outside in the open air, things are less warlike but every bit as intense. By the hedges, a couple of men go through the crowd of sunbathers going, "How are you, guy?" to strangers and clasping their hands. "Praise God, brother!" they cry to men they don't know, and "Bless you, man!" "Man, I'd like to share the glory of God with you," says a beautiful young man to a truck driver with a bushy beard. All I can think of is my gay male friends smiling at other men on the street and hooking up with them. There are lots of young sailors in uniform, including one shirtless looker wearing just the Stand in the Gap Bible stuffed down the back of his Navy whites.

"Our greatest sin is that we have forsaken your son as the consuming passion of our hearts!" I hear now from the stage. It's Joseph Garlington, in a romantic mode this time. "Men, I hold this against you. You have forsaken your first-love passion for Jesus Christ." Men cry out warmly at this. Garlington shouts that we need to have "a passion for his presence and a hunger for his word." He keeps repeating "first love" till I begin to think the Promise Keepers have transposed the old Adrienne Rich doctrine that all of us originally, and most properly, love women—transposed it, somehow, to the men in the family. Without this original homoerotic passion, we have "sexual immorality," Garlington says. It's a fascinating formula. First-love passion for Jesus makes you free from any lower-grade passions like adultery and oral sex with men. But we haven't lusted in our hearts enough yet for the Son of Man. "Christian men are addicted to pornography. Christian men are addicted to sexual abuse. Say, 'It's my fault.'" The crowd says, rapidly, "It's my fault." "Neil Sedaka talked about 'the tears through the hungry years.' There's an epidemic of STDs. There are 'seven gold lampstands,' like in Revelation 1:12. I'd like to ask you all to prostrate yourselves now, if you're physically able."

All around me on the dirty grass men obey. They put their faces on the ground in a very cramped space. Those who don't have the space bend over standing, in very painful-looking positions. "I'd like you to be silent like a dead man," Garlington bids us. Noiselessly, "I'd like you to first of all tell him of the love in your heart that is for him." It is so silent among these half million men that my pen on the paper is suddenly loud. In shame, men stick their butts up in the air, like Moslems praying to Mecca. Men are trying to weep without making any noise. "And now, I'd like you to privately and in your own hearts pray out a prayer to him of confession and brokenness, and how far you have gone from your own first love." The man next to me starts to moan, *"Oh, God!"* and make crazy little desperate noises that may or may not be tongues. Others sob with their need to just reach Him, mucus dribbling from their noses.

Animal sounds, repentance, and love all around me. Men shake with prayers full of their own unspeakable vileness, and their tender longing to be changed. There's so much desperation mixed up with their desire to be good, it's hard to listen to. Sometimes "being good" is only about the desire to be let back in. *If I obey, then he will love me.* But they also sound like they're repenting some real wrongs. It is ugly, beautiful, weird. "What we have done," Garlington says. "Our abuses. Giving. Getting." He tells the men to form groups of three, but "Don't talk. You can meet each other later. Don't talk, pray." I wish I could be in one of these huddles. The men look so vulnerable and sweet with each other, holding each other. "Say you are found in the name of Jesus!" one prays in the threesome nearest me. "Hallelujah, oh lord Jesus, give us the right mind, lord Jesus, bless their finances, bless their homes."

This kind of love is not enough, I see. The "first-love passion" of it all is wonderful but it lacks something; the "brokenness" and abandon and surrender are gorgeous but not enough, not nearly enough for real loving. If the only way to meet the Other is to do exactly what they want, what good is love? Later in the rally we chant "NO MORE ABUSE! NO MORE ABANDONMENT," which is wonderful, and we watch moving videos of fathers apologizing for abusing their children. Why, then, are we asked to tongue the dirt to win the love of our Father in Heaven? Why should a vow to stop abusing others require abusing ourselves? Does *someone* have to get abused for love to go on, to be shared?

These men seem to think so.

They really do want to be good; they are so fervent to be good that I sometimes want to kiss them. *"Let me just be a part of my household!"* I hear someone agonizingly pray among the rows of men, and "In Washington, in Boston, in New York, in every city and town, make a difference, Lord!" But their desire to be good is tied up with so many painful things that it often comes out incoherently. Their morality has little content, except abject need. And their love has little content but the same.

4

Parley

It's time for me to try to imagine a different way to connect to the religious right. Perhaps one where I'm not in drag at all.

℘

I am having coffee with Focus on the Family, the religious-right media-and-counseling mega-nonprofit, and it is sort of like having coffee with Barney, a television character I adore and most adults hate. Like the bubbly purple one, Focus is more influential than the Christian Coalition and about six times as sympathetic. The influential Focus men who have filed into this lovely conference room to have coffee with me are very nice behind their ties and their clean shaves: niceness, in so many ways, is what Focus is all about, and the reason you probably haven't heard of it, despite its power.

"Is it weird to be here?" Bobby Ace, a cute designer with dyed blond hair and good clothes, asks me kindly. "I know it would be hard for *me*." (When did the Christian right start dressing so well?) Allegedly nonpolitical, Focus says its purpose is to speak to the faithful and unfaithful alike who want their "home" to be "strengthened" and their "family" "assisted," as the group's mauve-colored secular-outreach handout puts it. "Helping You Build a Healthier Home . . . Practical Books That Meet Real Needs . . . We're Here to Help." The language of therapy and tenderness is there in almost every Focus publication (11 different magazines with circulations from 22,000 to 2 million, 10 different radio programs aired on 4,000 stations, videos, best-selling books, church bulletins and children's television programs). When people who need people read Focus-published books on parenting or call their professionally staffed counseling line, they can expect to hear not only diatribes against homosexuals and adults who masturbate, but also rather beautiful words about building more profound relationships, opening up to your emotions if you're a man, how to really be there for your children, and ways to take care of yourself when you're healing from family abuse or psychic pain.

I'd like my home strengthened. I'd be thrilled to be healed from my psychic pain. In fact, I'm a glutton for therapy (which has the same root meaning as *ministry,* it turns out: service, succor, assistance). That's why I love it when Focus magazines come in my mailbox. The day that *Brio* comes, the warm little Focus organ for teen girls is open and in my hands before I've even turned the TV on. I sit back and relax with it after the workday, reading the "Dear Susie" advice column ("Dear Susie: I was raped a few months ago by someone I really trusted. Since it wasn't my fault, I'm wondering if God still thinks of me as a virgin."), a feature on what to do if someone calls you "ugly" or "fatso" ("Think about what's behind it."), and an essay about fairy tales by a rather feminist sixteen-year-old reader ("You don't need a prince or a knight at all! And yet all the stories make the princess look like a weak, defenseless, fearful little thing who will faint if anyone so much as looks at her.").

Brio is comforting, fun, and only savage sometimes. Back when Debbie Gibson and Madonna were having a public debate about sex, *Brio* gave a fiction award to a teenage girl's story that presented their two positions accurately. "I agree with Madonna," character Cathy says. "It's my body. I should be able to do anything I want with it." But her friend Maria cracks open her Bible and quotes, *"'Your body is a temple of the Holy Spirit. . . . You are not your own property; you have been bought and paid for.'"* Slavery was, fascinatingly, presented as the better option for the *Brio* reader. Focus simultaneously tells people that homosexuals commit 68 percent of mass murders and that you should never tell your child she's a stupid, ugly moron, because she is a lovely, brilliant child of the light.

It's a little hard to take in both their kinds of messages at once.

℞

I've come to Focus on the Family before, but never as myself, the way I'm doing now. People often describe Focus as a wolf in sheep's clothing, but in those days, I was a jaunty wolf-in-wool myself whenever I went to meet the right. I felt like Superman, keeping my secret powers hidden till the final moment. The first time I came to Focus, I wore long white clip-on earrings that hurt my ears and I clapped when the woman at the Welcome Center put on a video that showed us gay men in leather threatening a tiny child's innocence.

Back then, Focus was headquartered downtown in Colorado Springs in a friendly, four-story building covered on the outside by pictures of Christmas presents, candy canes, cartoon characters, Jesus, and angels. It looked like a giant preschool. "Could I be taken care of here?" I wondered, ducking my head to get inside so I could see the film about the threat to children. Gay organizations never have candy canes or presents painted on their doors, much less tell you that your parents or Jesus will love you forever. I was more than a little bit jealous.

I resisted the compulsion I suddenly felt to remove my wig and reveal the butch haircut underneath, crying, "I am an angel sent by God! Homosexuals are angelic," and another strong temptation to fall on my knees, confess my sins, and join the happy Focus family.

Infiltration, hiding, disguise, the constant danger of conversion and the inescapable desire for it are dominant metaphors for both us and them, the religious right and the gay movement. And they're the burning core of our fantasies about each other, too. There are reasons besides pragmatic ones why ACT UP spent so much time crouching in the middle of religious-right rallies dressed as hidebound conservatives, reasons why Ralph Reed confessed to a preference for "paint[ing] my face and travel[ing] at night" and engaging in sexily secret forays where the enemy "don't know it's over till [they're] in a body bag."

In 1996 Reed looked deep into the eyes of a predominantly feminist, gay, and Jewish New York audience and purred, "I think it was Oscar Wilde who said that diplomacy is when you tell people they're going to hell in a way that makes them want to go there as quickly as possible." Drag always contains an element of fascination as well one of revulsion, and when Reed, the most undercover member of the religious right, quoted Oscar Wilde's words with flair, much more was going on than some audaciously cheeky wit.

He made me *want* to go there, like a shot. He also really turned me on. Lots of lesbians think that Reed looks like a soft butch lesbian, and I say they're exactly right. Little is sexier than an enemy who looks like you, particularly when he likes to dress like you, wants to "wear cammies and shimmer along on [his] belly" so that you never see him as he is, until he flicks the switchblade open like the beautiful hated brother in *Querelle*.

⁊

I've decided to do things differently when I come to Focus this time. After all these years, I'm sick of infiltrating, sick of relishing Michael Swift's tongue-in-cheek warning, "We are everywhere: we have infiltrated your ranks. Be careful when you speak of homosexuals, because we are always among you; we may be sitting across the desk from you; we may be sleeping in the same bed with you . . . You will be shocked and frightened . . . We shall sodomize your sons, emblems of your feeble masculinity, of your shallow dreams and vulgar lies . . . we will stab you in your cowardly hearts and defile your dead, puny bodies . . . Tremble, hetero swine, when we appear before you without our masks."

I'm sick of hoping that people tremble when they find out who I really am. Maskless and unprotected, I've come to the Focus complex at last because I've been very curious about what it would be like to meet these people as myself. Under my real name, I've arranged to interview three Focus writer-politicos who know exactly who I am and exactly what sort of thing I tend to write. This seems appropriate; I've come to Colorado Springs in the first place in order to give a talk called "The Intimate Enemy: Finding Myself in the Religious Right." It seems craven to profess intimacy with people I will never allow to see me as I am.

Clark Kent never finds any intimacy. I walk down Explorer Drive (a street name Focus would have had to invent if it had not been here already) and gaze out at the godly view of Colorado mountains enclosing much of the U.S. missile system, the sort of view groups like Focus put on a pamphlet when they want to evoke the Founding Fathers and their closeness to God's intent. Then, I enter Focus's big white doors. From the front, it looks like a highway Howard Johnson's, only infinitely cleaner, sweeter, and more stately. And I take a deep breath.

🍂

Everyone in upscale Howard Johnson's is extremely polite. A secretary offers me coffee and apologizes for the "mix-up" because of which Focus vice president Tom Minnery will be unable to meet with me. She proffers another vice president in his stead, Paul Hetrick, the veep of media relations. Larry Burtoft, Focus's resident "expert on homosexuality," does show. In place of my third requested date, Burtoft's boss, Focus has provided the cute young man, Bobby Ace, who works on Focus's periodicals.

Larry, a kind, rumpled man in his forties who looks younger, with the air of a sweet academic, brings copies of my articles. He's the author of a Focus report called *Setting the Record Straight: What the Research* Really *Says About the Social Consequences of Homosexuality*. Paul, a big, somewhat mournful man, is stiffer with me, but I know he's just itching to be warm. His suit is the real thing, the kind that Wall Street businessmen wear, but his belly pokes through it dejectedly. He has an air of sweat and sadness that makes me want to pat his hand.

Bobby Ace of the parti-color hair keeps his mouth shut after empathizing with me about the weirdness. I begin by asking about pornography; one of the most troubling things about Focus, to me, is its terror of fantasy. In a book segment called "Consequences of Experimentation," the head of Focus, James Dobson, writes of pornography that "the susceptible adolescent must simply crack the door an inch or two and a monster will run out and grab its wide-eyed victim." (For all I've said about the monster, I don't believe it comes from reading porn, or wanting sex.) The single most troubling Focus product is a video called *Sex, Lies, and the Truth*, in which nonmarital sex is literally depicted as a House of Horrors. Grotesque carnival barkers in the video become grotesque faces contorted in orgasm; as a nightmarish lover comes close enough to

almost kiss the camera with his revolting lips, the
voiceover tells us that sex will lead to emotional damage,
betrayal, and death.

Thinking about it can be just as bad. "Guard your mind
. . . guard your eyes," warns Promise Keeper Gary Oliver
in a Focus anthology. "The little Sunday School song has
some powerful wisdom for us":

> Oh be careful little eyes what you see.
> Oh be careful little ears what you hear.
> Oh be careful little lips what you speak.
> There's a Father up above, looking down in ten-
>   der love,
> Oh be careful little eyes what you see.

Why is Focus so afraid of what can be articulated,
wanted, seen?

"Obviously, as American citizens, we're all beholden to
the Constitution," Paul Hetrick says mildly. "Our concern
has not been to restrict porn, but to point out the problems
with it." It's not for nothing that he's the vice president for
media relations. Paul goes into an extended oration about
how public-policy questions are only a small part of
Focus's work, anyway; Focus spends a much greater portion of its time answering phone calls from people with
problems who call 1-800-AFAMILY or write Focus for
help.

"We get a lot of mail from women whose husbands are
addicted to pornography. The husband often wants to
involve her in things he's read about in porn." He passes
along the arresting information that "we hear from many

pastors' wives" whose husbands want them to do the equiv-
alent of getting on all fours, shaking their butts, and begging
for it while another man looks on. "Something like twenty-
eight percent of pastors are involved in using porn."

These people don't deny the plank in their own eye.
Bobby chimes in, "If you are prone to be addicted to
pornography—and I am, just like I'm prone to drugs, I did
coke—some people it's gonna grab and pull 'em in."

But what exactly is wrong with porn, anyhow, assum-
ing that you don't insist that your wife let you come in her
hair? "We don't think it's healthy for anyone, particularly
men, to saturate his mind with fantasies and ideas that
tend to put the woman on the plane of being an object,"
says Paul. "It's a misunderstanding on the part of the man
as to what his marital relationship is all about."

"And of course," says Larry, sounding grave, "there's
an extended concern that goes beyond the family, about
what pornography reflects about our society's view of
women." Pornography "is a very abstracting way of looking at a person—a way of reducing a person to a certain
physical ideal." I think of how much my gay male friends
would like to hear this, and how oppressed they all are by
the tyranny of buffness standards and youth-worship.
"Our perspective is that personhood is somewhat deeper
and more lasting than the body."

Yes, lots of porn *is* sexist and gross, and full of anger
toward women, toward men, and toward sexuality itself.
But so are lots of other things that people say, do, and
think—even evangelicals, even feminists, even me. Why
does pornography present such an intense danger, why is
the fantasy monster lurking behind the door? "We do not

regard sex as a monster," Paul says, a little impatiently. "We regard it on the contrary as one of the best gifts God has given us. We have a responsibility to use it in appropriate ways, and if we do, it is an enormous creative force." I feel my hackles rise at the word "appropriate." Who is to say what sort of sex is appropriate? But then Paul says: "What's wrong with porn is that people like Hugh Hefner are taking something that's special and a gift and the core of creative power and misuing it and making money on it."

I nod at him, surprised. What annoys me, too, about pornography is perhaps most of all its shoddiness: bad acting, bad writing, bad assumptions about the way sex has to be, often bad sex. Even the well-written porn that's emerged from the pens of gay and lesbian writers has been hampered by a very limited imagination, as though sex could only be one thing now that it had become a product. Only jaded and cutting in tone, or only sadomasochistic, or only the sort of thing *Homo Extra* says is hot.

What's wrong with porn, Larry says, is that it teaches us that sex is about "this image that has no uniqueness, has no character, is airbrushed." Though I like porn, I can only agree. What's wrong with porn is what is wrong with consumer culture in general—the reduction of sweet, funky, and intimate things to meaninglessness, the commodification of human life itself. If it's not written in the language of HOT! THROBBING! WOMANFLESH! you will not see it on the shelf.

The problem, of course, is that none of us can say with certainty what sex (or life) would look like, absent the culture of hype. It is both to my joy and my chagrin that I find out that my Focus friends and I share a disdain for commodity culture—because, amazingly, of what it does to our society's "values." "As we go roaring off into the next millennium," Larry harrumphs passionately, "look who's being trampled on and look who's getting abused. Look at what cost our financial success has come, and our onward and upward success, look who's getting victimized in the process."

I knew there was a reason I liked him. "I hope this doesn't offend you, but a lot of what Focus says sounds like Marxism to me," I tell Larry. "All this concern for the restoration of relationships, the restoration of people to their full humanity, in contradistinction to what ads, mass culture, and atomized jobs have made them become." I'm already talking like my memories of the early Marx, interspliced with the wussiest and sweetest members of the Frankfurt School.

"It's not by chance that Marxism is called 'the Christian heresy,'" says Larry, smiling. "It's not by chance that liberals who work out of a Christian tradition find Marxism to be a helpful tool of critique. Marx saw some things. He saw the alienation of the worker from the product of his labor. He saw what the industrial revolution did to family relationships. And any Christian who was really following Christ would weep with the Marxist about that alienation."

Paul isn't pleased with the turn the discussion has taken. "Marxism was very shortsighted in understanding human nature and how the Bible comes to grips with the things that are in the heart and soul of man," he announces. "I'm not offended when you compare us, but I think Marxism has given us a lot of negative examples and a lot of death."

Larry gets that he's gone a bit too far. "It misunderstands the root of social evil. It looks at material forces and doesn't look into the heart of the individual. But, you know, Marxists are right when they say that the problem isn't just 'a bunch of bad people.' We recognize that there *are* social forces." He's enjoying himself, and launches into a side issue about how Marxists were wrong that there can be "a pure class that will rise and govern everyone benevolently"—the very notion, I think to myself, that some Christian rightists have been promoting as the reason Christians ought to take over the school boards.

We talk about sex for what must be an hour of the three we spend together. I've never met men so concerned about their own potential to hurt others erotically. "Freedom is not the license to do whatever you want. Freedom is the power to do what you ought," Paul tells me pleadingly. "Because not everything I want is good! Some of the things I want to do will hurt other people!" It's strangely moving to hear his fear of his own cravings. I think of my dear friend Richard Goldstein and the cap he used to wear that said PROTECT ME FROM WHAT I WANT.

I don't tell these men that I myself have been trying to read porn and have fantasies that are vanilla, not S/M. (I stopped doing S/M, too, whereas I once thought it would save me.) It's not that I think S/M hurts people or is evil; I just realized it was preventing me from having other kinds of sex and love that I wanted more. But for someone who says that desire itself is always beneficial, I'm in a bit of a logical bind.

"We don't think the thought-life is disconnected to the actual lived life," Larry says. "The thought-life has an impact that is as important—well, it's not *as* important—but from our perspective, it's the source of what a man will be. Christ was very clear about that." He's right: Jesus really did say that "bad" feelings and desires are just as bad as bad *actions* (which makes me wonder exactly why anyone saw him as compassionate). "We believe the thought-life ought to be protected."

"Not protected by Focus on the Family!" Paul interjects quickly.

"Not protected by Focus on the Family!" confirms Larry. "It ought to be protected by the individual."

The Focus folks are in a logical bind about desire, too. "I would not agree with the evangelical who tries to zip sex up and put it in a locked box inside another locked box and lock it up in a closet somewhere," Paul tells me. Larry adds: "It's not that you shouldn't have sexual thoughts." Bobby interrupts: "It's how you're gonna *control* them!" Paul concludes on an appropriately ambiguous note: "It's not fantasy that's evil . . . it's *unbridled* fantasy." In *Children at Risk*, Dobson says that pornography is a "progressive" addiction that leads to ever more horrific reading materials, including depictions of "sodomy," "sex between women and bulls, stallions or boars," and eventually to horrific *behaviors*, including rape and serial murder. Ted Bundy, Dobson says, was launched on his murderous career by "the accidental discovery of 'girlie magazines' at a roadside dump." But Paul claims evangelicals are falsely portrayed as overfearful about sex. "We never said that if you go down to the drugstore and buy a *Playboy*, you're gonna turn into Ted Bundy."

They are certainly speaking out of both sides of their mouths. The question is, am I? How do you deal with the darkness within you without repressing it and at the same time, without feeding it? Leaving aside that the Focus guys and I would identify very different sorts of things in a person as "darkness," don't you have to acknowledge the darkness in you if you don't want to be completely overwhelmed by it? "That's a Scriptural idea, Donna," Larry says a little smugly. "If you do not acknowledge the sin in you, the dark places in you, you are not only a liar, you are in a sense in bondage to the dark forces."

Though we don't see homosexuality as any kind of evil, this idea is also the driving ideology of gay liberation. If you don't acknowledge this hidden, forbidden impulse, it will overwhelm you; if you don't acknowledge it, you will be forever in bondage to it, whether this takes the form of a loveless life, compulsive heterosexuality, or unrestrainable homophobia culminating in violence.

In the gnostic Gospel of Thomas, Jesus says: "If you bring forth what is within you, what you bring forth will save you. If you do not bring forth what is within you, what you do not bring forth will destroy you."

It is a beautiful idea, and in so many ways it is true. Every person has in them sadistic rage, profound hurt, sexual arousal, and the need to be loved; each of these feelings must be acknowledged and accepted to some degree, or it will indeed destroy us. Each of these feelings, not coincidentally, has some expression in the world of porn and personal sexual fantasy, which is, among other things, a great way to at least temporarily accept one's least acceptable feelings.

But what this model fails to take into account is the *other* way desire works, not through repression but through stimulation. It is "vanity," Foucault said, "to go questing after a desire that is beyond the reach of power. . . . Where there is desire, the power relation is already present. . . . The idea of a rebellious energy that must be throttled [is] inadequate for deciphering the manner in which power and desire are joined to one another." In other words, there is an important sense in which sexual desires and other private cravings are not "private" at all, but social; *not* about the inborn nature of the individual, but about the cravings incited by the family and the culture.

"My wife yells and screams, because in her family that was the only way of being heard," Bobby shares. "But we talk about it afterwards. You can feed the fire or you can try to put the fire out. . . . I don't agree with dwelling on these urges, fantasizing about them, but I don't agree with 'Don't think about it, deny it,' either, which is where too many are at in this ministry."

How do we articulate our own experience? How do we know what things about ourselves can and cannot be changed? When the newly-come-out Ellen DeGeneres went on *Oprah* with her new lover, Anne Heche, I was watching with a roomful of lesbians who became scandalized by Heche's accounts of her own process—especially her assertion that she "was not gay" until she met the star of *Ellen*. Heche reported that their "souls connected" during their first exchange of glances across a crowded room, that she felt "love" for DeGeneres only weeks after meeting her, and this experience was how she'd come to feel desire for women. The lesbians I was watching with were furious with Anne Heche because she told a *different* story than the one that has become a mainstay of current-day gay and lesbian culture. Her story made them uneasy because it emphasized romantic love, not inborn sexual feelings; fluidity of sexual desire, not discovery of one's unchangeable nature (an equally romantic notion, when you think about it).

People desire what they are told not to, but they also desire what they're told to. An attraction to men is the dark secret of many lesbians, just as feelings for the same sex are buried deep within the hearts of many heterosexuals; one culture's dutiful sexual duty is another's scandal. If you're told often enough that you should like only a certain gender, chances are you will; if you're told often enough that you're a juicy little slut, that's what you'll think you are; and if you tell yourself that you're hateful and disgusting, hateful and disgusting at least in some measure you will be. Desire doesn't just bubble up from our loins, it is endlessly redirected by the interaction of history, power, and our minds.

I was much more passionate about wanting to do S/M when I read only S/M porn, thought S/M was my "inner nature," bought whips, and pursued a romantic S/M relationship with a very loving young woman who gave me military regalia. (As Althusser says, paraphrasing Pascal: "Kneel down, move your lips in prayer, and you will believe.")

Perhaps no social movement has fully acknowledged that desire is a dialectic; it is both about "who we are" and *not* about "who we are." As with emotional responses (including religious feeling and, very likely, political commitment), we choose it and it chooses us.

If it's hard to tell where our "darkness" comes from, it's equally hard to know the source of our "light"—the things we believe will save us. Focus's agenda of helping people in pain isn't just cheap icing it throws on to distract us from its right-wing cake; its right-wing goals and nurturing agenda are one. "Many of the young women who go into porn have been sexually abused," Paul tells me grimly. I already know, and I add inwardly that most of the men have been, too. Paul's agenda on pornography is very different from mine, but our concern for people who've been molested seems to be just about as intense. I often pause in the middle of watching porn videos because I'm ambivalent about watching the actresses re-enact the circumstances of their abuse. Probably they believe that it will bring them to truth.

A beaming secretary brings us more coffee and gently shuts the door behind her. Bobby Ace gulps some liquid courage and starts asking me eager, curious questions about my book. When I say that it's about the intimate relationship between the evangelical movement and the gay movement, Bobby has his own things to tell me about that relationship. "You should include a third group in your book, the ex-gay movement. 'Cause they're evangelical *and* they're gay. That's what I came out of, too, and probably why I'm here to speak the news to you today. And there are all kinds of biblical reasons and causes why

I had those impulses in me. The Bible says, 'The sins of the father shall be visited on the son, even unto the third and fourth generation.' My dad's dad was a wife-beater and an abuser, and me, I was working at *Men's Fitness,* a magazine with a pretty gay audience. My grandad took my father out to the barn and fondled him and showed him how to have sex with a cow."

I'm still trying to grok the fact that Bobby has just come out to me—about several different things at once. But he goes on coming out endlessly, in an uninterrupted stream: "Around the time that I came out, a man came up to me and said. 'You have been deceived, and you shall deceive.' I ran into J.R.'s. Then it happened to me again, the same stupid words—in church, the text was, 'You have been deceived, and you shall deceive.' I couldn't handle it. I really wanted my sin. I cried because I wanted my sin. My best friend and I agreed to come out of the lifestyle at the same time, 'cause we figured the gays would hate us *and* the evangelicals would hate us, but if we had one friend to walk through life with, it would be okay."

His fear of being hated by everyone is rather poignant to me. They're hard, those desperate days when you worry about not even having "one friend to walk through life with" once people find out what you're really like. Bobby'd had a hard time finding love. And he lived in the extra-vapid Hollywood/Chelsea, gay-male party scene I personally have always identified as a type of hell. "At *Men's Fitness,* there were a lot of beautiful models, and a lot of drugs. I was a coke addict. I'd been in the lifestyle five years, and I was suicidal. I could not find happiness. I could not find a lasting relationship."

But change is growth, and growth is life. Bobby was given several signs from God that he could change. "My dad went back to the Lord, and he quit smoking. The fact that he was able to quit smoking shamed me a little. It made me think, If he can do this, I should be able to quit the lifestyle. They say that if you draw closer to God, God will draw closer to you." About two weeks after he prayed for a change, "a loud thought came into my head. *'Call Focus on the Family! Call Focus!'* I thought, if it's the Lord, maybe there'll be a job." There was: Bobby is now the designer for a Focus serial for teen boys. (Focus had no idea he was gay when they hired him. Every month, there are enormous phallic symbols on the cover.)

Bobby wasn't alone in seeing Focus as both potential employer and potential saviour. Later, Paul tells me that a lot of the staff became acquainted with Focus for the first time when "they had some situation in their home or life that was difficult and they called Focus for help. A lot of the people I know in Focus h. v: really been in brokenness." (Sometimes the aid Focus gives to people who reach out and touch them is material. The organization doles out $1.9 million to individuals who ask for it each year.)

"There's something out there trying to reach people," Bobby says, "and there's also something out there trying to reach people to destroy them." Sometimes things are both at once, or attempts at one that accomplish the other. All sorts of nurturing interventions fit this bill. Some parental love, for example, like his grandad's for his dad. Sexual abuse itself is a means of communication, a reaching out of sorts—for the abuser, and sometimes even the victim, a means of violent communion and a nexus of ambiguous love. Bobby himself may have been the source of such communion for someone as a child; it isn't entirely clear. He refers to "a lot of the things that women did to me as a kid" and the resultant "stuff" he's had to "work through" with his wife about it: "So that when a woman's holding me around the stomach, something goes, 'danger!' 'danger!' 'The Devil's gonna jump on me!'"

When love gets mixed with something entirely different, more than one generation *is* always affected. To that extent, the Bible words are right, though they are hardly fair. "Growing up, my dad was poor, fifty cents was like a hundred dollars to him, and lots of gay guys wanted to feed him. And my dad thought he might be gay. I think that's why my dad didn't hug me. In pictures, he's always holding us real distant from him, 'cause he didn't know what was perverted and what wasn't."

It's not always easy to tell, for Bobby or anyone else. When he became an ex-gay, "music died for me," Bobby says. "I love Barbra Streisand. (Didn't we all!) God, the girl can sing! But look at the stuff in her life that I disagree with! And I think her son is gay! And I think, why isn't she praising the Lord for all her gifts?" In one breath, he talks of loving feelings for his best friend, Ed, and how, when Ed fell ill recently with Lou Gehrig's disease, "it hurt so much just thinking about it." In the next, he says of same-sex love, "It has never brought me anything but a temporary fix, like a shot up my nose."

I say to Bobby, "It sounds to me like you were looking for healing, and for a way to make your relationships better. Why did you think you had to give up same-sex love for that to happen, instead of working on, say, addiction or relationship issues?"

"I don't *like* the things He's changed in my life. But the thing is to walk in the path He wants for me, not the path I want. The trick is to do the kind of thing *He* wants for me."

"He" sounds, yet again, like an abusive lover. I'll let you heal if you give up sexual fulfillment! I'll nurture you if you completely ignore your own wants! But then Bobby says, "He exposes me gradually, day by day, to the things in my life He wants me to work on, while He's giving me the power to correct it. He's not ripping the veil off all at once." Except that she would never say that I needed her to "give" me power, now Bobby's God sounds a little bit like my shrink.

His stories about homosexuality have the air of the parables of twelve-step groups, as interpreted by an eight-year-old. "I went jogging with a gay friend of mine in Hollywood. There's a bar there that closes at seven or eight in the morning, and they're all pilin' out of there with their shirts off, all these built-up guys. I look forward! My friend looks at them and can't stop looking. And he falls forward right on his face. I believe that was one of those moments God gave him. And I said to him, 'Anthony, *you're* the one that can't stop looking. *You're* the one that's in bondage.'"

Paul and Larry have been looking at their watches. Their junior colleague has been going on for forty minutes, taking it upon himself to tell me everything I might possibly desire to know about him, and often repeating especially dramatic tidbits, like the one about the time his friends went to New York Gay Pride the same weekend he and Ed attended a Christian event in Oakland. ("Bobby, what did *you* do this weekend? . . . [*catty voice:*] *Oh, so now you judge us?!*") The pièce de résistance is probably the one about "Mom's third open-heart surgery," which occurred recently, and meant that "Dad for the next year could not have sex with Mom. So he told me that he said to himself, 'I'll just go masturbate with these magazines,' but Mom would sleep on these recliner chairs, she would nod off, so Dad knew it was a sign and he threw away all of his pornography. Mom couldn't do *anything*. But Dad said, 'Bobby, I will love her even if we never have sex again.'"

"Take it off," I want to growl at Bobby, "baby, take it all off!" I might pretend that Bobby is the only slut in this conversation, but really, I'm getting off on his story as much as he is. He seems to like reciting multicharacter scenes of shame and deliverance. 1) His family: "There was a lot of alcohol, a lot of arguing, and a lot of smoking, and my father was addicted to pornography!" 2) Other kids: "They would always call me 'Faggot' and 'Devil,' and maybe that's why I became it!" 3) His own rococo feelings about gay people: "I've been to lesbian bars, and they were even scarier than the men's bars. And I once read about a drag queen that killed someone. . . . But Ed and I loved our gay friends even more after we left the lifestyle, because we saw that God loved *us*, the trashy things that we were!"

Like a lot of people who talk to reporters, Bobby enjoys having an audience—enjoys it deliriously, rapturously. He ejaculates his story like someone on a talk show; on the whole, this is *not* like twelve-step, but like something far more unconscious and fevered. There's something almost sexual about his excessive testimony, like Whitman's: "I do not ask who you are . . . that is not important to me, / You can do nothing and be nothing but what I will infold you. / . . . . Mine is no callous shell, / I have instant conductors all over me whether I pass or stop, / They seize every object and lead it harmlessly through me. / . . . I hear the trained soprano. . . . She convulses me like the climax of my love-grip. . . . / I dote on myself. . . . There is that lot of me, and all so luscious. . . . "

And yet I understand his dilemma. Being sexually abused makes you want to pour yourself out on people, "adorning myself to bestow myself on the first that will take me," as Whitman wrote, "scattering it freely forever." It makes it hard to have relationships, and it makes you eager to be saved, by any means necessary. It can make someone dive into the gay party scene, and then dive back out into Christian heterosexuality. It makes you want to name yourself publicly, and then take on a new name. It makes you want to be baptized. It makes you want to be anointed. It makes you want to be touched and cared for

—I, too, can be excessive, like Bobby, so stop me before I get too rococo. "Victim, schmictim," some of my readers are saying at this juncture. They're sick of hearing about it, and in a certain way, they have a point. Truth to tell, we are *all* victimized in different ways, and in this strange culture of ours, *everyone's* feelings of victimization get sexualized like Bobby's. That is one reason Americans love to go on talk shows. (It is also why we ridicule people who do. On the whole, it is much easier to pretend to be above the fray.) "Christianity means giving up your life," Bobby confides. "My wife is beautiful, but not like, Oh, I just have to have it every night. I guess you could say we have intimacy without sexual intimacy." In his desire to blurt and convert, Bobby is probably many people's brother. In his difficulty with relationships, and in the trouble he has bringing sex and intimacy together, he is the brother of many people I know, gay and straight, sexually abused or not.

"When I came out, I felt great for a while," he says. Of course he did; because coming out as gay and coming out as ex-gay both proclaim the soul in newness to the world. Whatever Bobby's initial fears about "leaving the lifestyle," both experiences also hook you up with a community of people who welcome you with a sort of automatic warm regard—people who consider you their brother or sister, whether or not you are like them in any way. Bobby met his wife-to-be, Wanda, and most of his current friends at Focus on the Family. Wanda and he drive in to work together each morning, play soccer together, and get prayed on by other Focusoids at night. (How different is this, really, from the phenomenon known as lesbian-until-graduation, where women undergraduates come out as lesbians for four years to enjoy their college's lesbian community and then reenter the happy world of heterosexuality?)

Despite its sexual shortcomings, Bobby's relationship with Wanda appears to be one of the most meaningful relationships Bobby has ever had with anybody. The two Christian media mavens work hard on their friendship; they talk about everything; they get to the bottom of their problems (at least the problems that have nothing to do with being Christian conservatives). "She had never known anyone gay but me. She was from a pretty straight background—*she thought!*" Bobby laughs. He clued her in to family members that were his compatriots. When they started dating, they negotiated kissing and other erotic touches. "I said, Wanda, I've never been able to stop at kissing. But then I learned that for Wanda, kissing was as much or more pleasurable than sex."

They worked out Bobby's "issues" around certain touches by women. (Like many Christian men influenced by the Promise Keepers, Bobby has an "accountability partner," another man with whom he shares personal problems like this one that get in the way of his relationship with his wife. Bobby's partner also helps him deal with Wanda's yelling.)

Then there was the sensitive issue of Bobby's HIV status. "For about eight months to a year, we didn't even kiss," Bobby says. "I would not kiss her till she knew. But she said, 'If we're gonna do this, let's get on with it'—she meant, basically, before you die." Bobby, who has been diagnosed with AIDS, apparently thought he was at death's door, too; this may have been one of the reasons he "became ex-gay." "I said, Please, God, do not change me on my deathbed."

God changed Bobby long before that pass. "And she was willing to marry me, willing to give up children, willing to put herself at risk."

Put herself at risk? Before I can quite lose myself to visions of Wanda getting infected for the glory of God, Bobby assures me that he and Wanda have never had unsafe sex. "I would not do anything without protection and gels. And our pastor, during the private part of our ceremony, said to me, 'One of your vows is to protect her. Never, ever do not use protection.' But condoms have broken a couple of times for us. There is no such thing as safe sex.

"Right now," be that as it may, "we're practicing abstinence," Bobby informs me. "We do a lot of loving, hugging, kissing, and talking." He claims that "we were having fun making love. There were no problems there. But she was working on booklets at Focus that mentioned how small the virus is." Presumably, there were mental images of it sashaying through tiny condom holes. "That probably scared her the most. And I always said to her, 'Wanda, you will always be the one who chooses [about sex]. If you say no, it will be no.'" Now, therefore, they are brother-and-sister soul mates. "We do everything together, from working out at the gym to driving in together to Focus, going out to movies and dinner." I know gay male couples whose relationship is much the same. "We love each other and cuddle all the time, but he feels like my brother," one friend told me. "The sex part was over for us a long time ago."

Bobby doesn't sound a bit unhappy. "The weird part is, I feel sexually fulfilled without having sex! But I didn't know about Wanda. So I asked her—I said, I need to know so I don't give out misinformation." (Apparently, Bobby frequently puts out public updates on the state of his and Wanda's sex life.) "She said, 'Bobby, I feel sexually fulfilled, too.' We talk about it now and then—'Oh, I wish we could do this!' But there's more to life than sex. In the lifestyle, you'd be going out with someone and within a week or two, I was going, Next! With Wanda, there may be some temptations out there, but I have never felt like going, Next!"

Part of me is horrified by Bobby's choice to give up men. But another part of me is less willing to judge. I am moved by the intimacy he's built up with Wanda, even though it makes me want to cry that he thought he could not do this and be sexual at the same time. (Although I shouldn't be too quick to judge *that*, either. Bobby may have felt some genuine sexual feelings for Wanda, as tons of queer-identified people have felt for the other sex throughout history.) The point is, he shouldn't have felt required to choose between intimacy and homosexuality. Or—given his and Wanda's current state of abstinence—between intimacy and sexuality, period. But Bobby did feel so required to choose. More than that, it seems, he *wanted* to choose. I'm sure that the fact that Wanda was outside his usual boundaries of lust made it far easier for him to love her—not less.

"Ex-gays" aren't the only people who make this choice—not by a long shot. And they are certainly not the only people who feel pressed to. My most profound relationship at this moment is a platonic friendship with a gay man whom I love very much. I very much want to have a relationship with a lover that is just as trusting, just as intimate, just as long-term as this friendship is—but right now, I don't. Plain old intimacy is hard enough, for most people. An intimacy that is just as profound sexually as it is emotionally (or vice versa) is, for many of us, nearly impossible.

It is not just those of us whose affairs are short-lived who have trouble bringing sex and intimacy together; it is a culturewide phenomenon, from the lesbian couples caught in "lesbian bed death" to the heterosexuals disturbed to find that their partner no longer feels like the Marvell lines "the luscious clusters of the vine / Upon my mouth do crush their wine / The nectarine, and curious peach / Into my hands themselves do reach" after twenty years of marriage. The fruit on the Tree of Life that the angel guards from us with his flaming sword is not immortality, but sex and intimacy, combined. Some people have it, it is true, but as Blake wrote, "Every Night and every Morn / Some to Misery are Born. / Every Morn and every Night / Some are Born to sweet delight. / Some are Born to sweet delight. / Some are born to Endless Night."

But even people who don't have it can be happy, Hollywood and *Maurice* notwithstanding. "It got harder with us as we got closer," Bobby tells me. "Yet I realized, yes, I've messed up my life, but I have not messed up with Wanda." Good for him, I want to say; too bad that he's absorbed poisonous messages about homosexuality, too bad that sex is so hard for him, but good for him for making such a wonderful friendship. I'm a little shocked at my own attitude toward Bobby, the first "ex-gay" I've ever had a coffee with. But no situation is ever entirely hellish, and no identity is completely unredeemed. How can I hate Bobby? I am so much like him. I am determined to live in the orchard, and I'm not giving up the struggle (as, ultimately, he has). But my challenges are similar.

Paul finally interrupts Bobby's autobiography and my secret sharing of it. "It's a privilege for us to have someone who holds your views here," he tells me soberly. "What is it about us that people on the progressive side fear?" He really wants to know. "Is it that we're gonna take over America city by city, and force our views on America?"

That's an interesting supposition. I tell him many people fear that, but I personally am more worried by the religious right's efforts to fight laws that protect gay people from discrimination.

Bobby says, "I agree with Amendment Two on the point that special rights should not be granted to you, to me, to anyone. You don't deserve special rights because you're gay."

I ask whether it ought to be possible to fire people because they're gay (which Amendment Two would have allowed). Bobby says petulantly, "I can be fired because I'm a Christian."

In the pandemonium of voices that breaks out, I don't get a chance to tell him he is actually protected from that fate by the Constitution. Quivering to speak, Larry desires me to know that on Amendment Two, "Focus restrained itself. The issues of Amendment Two was going on before we got here. We did not tell people to vote for Amendment Two. We only had one show about it before the vote, and that was only aired in Colorado." And besides, the wench is dead. "The show was just to help people in our community understand the amendment. And the only other thing we did was give Colorado for Family Values [the group sponsoring the amendment] a gift-in-kind of about eight thousand dollars to create commercials. We reported that as a political contribution." He seems pretty defensive for someone who has not been rebuked.

All three of my new friends seem profoundly scared of being accused of doing hurtful things to gays. "We didn't do that [give CFV a gift] because we thought gays should be able to be kicked out of their jobs and apartments," Larry continues. "That was not the idea on our part at all. We did not believe that gays should not have a job." Too bad. They supported the anti–civil rights amendment because, Larry says, "there's a move out there in the gay community that isn't content with that, that wants further legitimation."

Hurriedly, he opens a new can of worms. "There's people saying, 'I was born this way and it is as inappropriate for people to sit in judgment of me as it would be for me to sit in judgment of heterosexuals.' But gay biology, we don't think that's been proven . . ."

"I don't think it's been proven, either. I think gay biology theory is pretty clearly wrong."

Larry smiles, looking like a shocked cat that's just been offered the canary with no struggle. But I haven't given his side anything of value. Have I?

The origins of homosexuality have nothing to do with questions about its morality. They have even less to do with the question of civil rights. Why is it so scary, then, that *Larry* thinks I've given him a weapon? Is it because I am sitting at a table with three homophobes, passing the sugar to people I am not even supposed to be in the same room with without screaming? Am I devaluing my friendliness, my conversation, and my smarts by offering them to this *treyf*?

In our conversation, which is still going on, Larry and Paul are still breaking their necks to convince me they are not homophobic. "Do we have a right to say we're gonna drive you out of our neighborhoods?" Paul asks rhetorically. ("Where would they go?" Larry wonders in an aside.) Paul continues: "Or something worse, like what happened to the Jews in the 1930s? To the extent that someone brings that kind of hatred and abuse, we would not support that at all," he says fiercely. He goes further: "If someone brings in passages from Leviticus where homosexuals were stoned, they're wrong. Because if you're gonna be consistent, you'd have to stone people for eating the wrong food, or eating on the wrong day. That was before Israel had the Revelation."

What an odd sensation. I don't believe I've ever heard a right-wing Christian say that kind of thing about Leviticus before. It feels pretty great. But on the other hand, all he is saying is that gays and lesbians should not be stoned or sent to the gas chambers. It's not all *that* magnanimous of him. I think that Larry, Paul, and Bobby are unconsciously aware of this, because within seconds they're back to singing the repetitious "We're Not Homophobic" song, even though I haven't even gotten a chance to open my mouth to say they are. "The idea that, as the Supreme Court said, you can only be motivated by animus if you disagree [that gay people should be protected from discrimination]," says Larry, "that's almost unanswerable." Indeed. "All you can say is, 'I'm not.'"

He is terribly upset by the fact that "a lot of people have this idea" that if you don't support equal rights, "you are a hate-filled bigot, you are a homophobe."

This is surely one of the strangest conversations I have ever taken part in. On the one hand, I enjoy hearing their guilt, and also hearing the odd comment that I have the deepest sympathy with, like Larry's suggestion that gay activists denounce opposition to gay rights on *moral* grounds ("Then we'd have an honest argument on the table"). Unlike the Focusoids, I don't think there's anything wrong with being filled with "hate"; all of us are, from time to time, and the immorality is not ever in *feeling* what remains an essentially irrational emotion, but in the actions we may take because we do.

On the other hand, it is fundamentally wrong to say *and* do the things that Larry, Bobby, and Paul do about gay people. Morally wrong, in the most profound way. (But I find myself wanting to judge even their *thoughts* on this subject as immoral. Who but a bigot could believe that a loving, rational, completely benevolent God would want to roast people for anything as innocent as homosexuality? If they were more concerned about fighting bigotry, they would reject their own dogma.) (Tiny Pat Buchanan subplot as this argument goes forward: Even Pat is doing what's he's doing "because he thinks he's fighting evil," I say magnanimously. But Paul frowns. "Except . . . some of his anti-Semitic tributaries bother me," he says. "He talks about the 'amen corner of Israel,' and I don't think I can back someone like that.")

Yet I'm surprised to find that I respect these people, the purveyors of disgusting filth like Amendment Two. It cannot be easy to sit in a closed room with the other side's journalist for hours and think aloud about your own shortcomings. "I feel that part of my mission in life is to protect either gays or ex-gays from the church," Bobby tells us. Larry, speaking about his own book on homosexuality, says, "There's a lot of things that I wish I had done differently. . . . There's a lot that's wrong with it."

In a letter he sends after our interview, Larry apologizes just in case he might have offended me by hugging me when I left. "It felt both awkward and right at the same time," he writes. "But if you experienced it as an inappropriate violation of your space, I am sorry." It is awkward, but touching, to get this strange little apology.

I did not, at all, Larry, experience it as an inappropriate violation of my space (or even an appropriate violation). Larry, if you're still participating in this perverse conversation by reading this, your hug was both awkward and right at the same time. Amendment Two and the Hyde Amendment were inappropriate violations. Nothing in our conversation was.

I don't know why, but it feels so liberating that I don't have to hate them at every moment and in every way. In the peace and openness of this klunky exchange, it's as though I've taken a knife out of my own *kishkes,* not theirs. How can you ever meet the Stranger unless you approach them without a weapon?

Given the warmth that I really do feel for them, it is odd to hear the Focus boys say things like "I can appreciate someone in your position who is honest and refers to sexual self-definition. When I testified at the state senate hearing up in Denver on same-sex marriage, I used an argument very much like that." It is not just odd, but infuriating, to hear Larry remark brightly that "To the extent that homosexuality emerges from a dysfunctional and abusive home life, Bobby is a testament that you can come out of that confusion." Or when Bobby whines, "I'm against your having special rights that I don't have."

I get angry.

Larry and Paul had been saying this endless riff about how Jesus combined "grace and truth," how he'd told the woman he'd just saved from stoning, "Neither do I condemn you. Go and sin no more." "He doesn't just say, 'I won't condemn you, see you later!'" Paul says, excited. "He says 'sin no more'! Nor does he just say, 'sin no more' without that other part, 'I don't condemn you.'" They've been telling me this to shed some light on how they see their work in Focus ("Unfortunately, one thing you can't do too well with grace is institutionalize it," admits Larry) and particularly, their work on homosexuality and gay rights. To me, this is not an adequate defense of indefensible actions. And as always, I'm ambivalent about the annoyingly, multivalently, and endlessly paradoxical gestures of Jesus Christ. Yet this turns out to be the absolute best time to take a leaf from his book.

I get very angry, and I tell them so. But I still feel loving. "I really love you guys," I start to tell Larry, Paul, and Bobby warmly, "but I just really hate your sin!"

Probably no gay or lesbian activist has ever told them this before. "Thanks," they say, as though I've done them a favor. How weird, these people are happy that I hate their sin. And they call people like me perverse?

"What *is* our sin?" asks Larry earnestly, as though he really wants to know.

I get heated, telling them what gay-rights laws actually do and how discrimination actually exists plentifully all around us. "Your fighting gay rights is wrong. . . . Straight people are explicitly protected under all existing gay-rights laws. There's no such thing as 'special rights'!"

My three adversaries admit to me that they are probably sinners toward gay people (though not specifically in terms of the antidiscrimination laws that I have mentioned). Still, I feel what I can only describe as divine grace—as an incalculable gift from Somewhere—that I have gotten to tell these men my anger in person and across a table from them, not two thousand comforting miles away from here, in published writing. Or, just as safe, screaming it to them across a barricade separating our mutually antagonistic rallies, armies to whom nothing alien is ever human.

Getting to tell these men my "wrath," as Blake would put it, means that I can also love them without fear. I hear Kurt Cobain in my head, asking someone to come as she is, as she is, as I finish telling them how immoral their anti-gay propaganda is. "As a tramp, as a friend," he sings joyfully to a potential lover. "No, I don't have a gun! No, I don't have a gun!"

5

The Gates

I am kneeling in a dark, enclosed space, kneeling under Sara's clavicle as I think about how to get what I want. I am licking her clavicle, steadying her hipbone, whispering to her about monsters, straight people, assaults. We are here to conquer ourselves and that is why I have to lead up to this slowly. It will be tolerable until it is intolerable, and then I will force my way past all bolts and ambivalences until, violating every wall, I force her and myself to feel it! The walls and bars themselves are sexy, part of the mystery and the dark, the unbreakable silence. There is no other way. I am so afraid of not feeling it.

That's only part of it. The other part is more fun, as I remember. Tearing Brenda's shirt because I am sick of her teasing, the great pleasures of hearing my hand smack against Sara's baby-soft ass like a vulnerable drum, pulling women's hair as I pull their nipples up and down, torturing and seducing all at once, everything I didn't get to do as a child and always wished I had.

And there's more: the eroticization of everyday life, images of myself caressing brooms and pincers in the hardware store. Going wild in Macy's Cellar, piling up basters, wooden spoons, and soft white cheeses I can spread on Rachel's ample bosom. Feather dusters, shaving cream, shoehorns! I feel like Walt Whitman in some ecstasy of commodity fetishism, testing loofahs against the side of my neck and biting-hot mustard against my endless desire. World without end, all in my hands! One of the things I like the most about S/M is the way it eroticizes *everything*, all stories and all potential stories, everything at once. Politics! Patrick Swayze! Teens with acne! All objects, and everything that can be imagined as an object. Bad insurance salesmen! Girls who love sleazy insurance salesmen with their badly tailored suits and moth-eaten ties!

In New York's Grand Hyatt hotel, in the middle of the most enamored summer of my life, I'm salivating in the Marketplace at the International S/M Leather Fetish Celebration, the largest sadomasochists' event in history. It is June of 1994, and three thousand of the people who most perfectly embody Foucault's happy notion of "perverts" have come together in these gold-painted halls for an extravaganza timed to coincide with the twenty-fifth anniversary of the Stonewall Riots. This is the apex of queerness, the heterosexuality of most participants notwithstanding; sadomasochism, even when practiced by straights, is broadly "queer" in the sense of resisting all the laws of sex that have been laid down for us. The political and cultural movement that has developed around S/M has profound connections to the gay movement. Like gay celebrations, this is a festival about desire taken out of bounds.

In the Marketplace, I go out of control just moving objects from one hand to the other, feeling and weighing everything that is available. There are miles of whips, red, black, green, silver, made of every possible material, horsehair, rubber, metal. There is so much more here than I ever imagined I could have, the soft, hard, stinging slap of a sleek doeskin whip I buy—my first—the eyes of my lover on me in ardor as I buy it, ripe breasts under clinging rubber like a bunch of grapes, a lustrous abundance of which I expected to be deprived.

There is room in this place for wooden fraternity paddles, magical garments that make their owners look like superheroes, the sexy sight of a near-naked woman on a leash gripped by a man, a throne you can buy, a man hopping around in a beautiful red straitjacket, looking happier than I've ever seen a man look ("We're taking a bathroom break," his lady friend sniggers, yanking him).

Every impulse unadmitted to consciousness is admitted here—and loved. The joy of finding a partner whose face I can slap, the desire to punish every cunt that turns you on, the fantasy of being Mephistopheles in his shining boots, the fantasy of being a batterer. If S/M people are right, the prince of darkness really *is* a gentleman; each of the many egregiously unpleasant elements in S/M carries with it an equal (and often cloaked) share of beauty. Many garments and objects in this room are too beautiful for the workaday world; they would be thought outlandish and excessive quite apart from their status as instruments of cruelty and humiliation. There are gleaming, tight suits for adults who want to look like Batman, like figures out of the

Arabian Nights, like medieval princes and Egyptian gods. Jana, a girl whom I knew in the sixth grade, struts around the sales tables like a glorious action figure, an alien warrior-spokesmodel in form-fitting, blue-black rubber accentuating her tightly packed muscles, like a beautiful insect just arrived to enslave us.

The objects for sale are made of materials that caress the hand too much, call too much attention to themselves, are too expensive. Never have I spent so much money for the sake of eros as I do now, giving the child ragamuffin inside me gifts of fur-lined bondage cuffs, antique men's shaving brushes with mean but feathery bristles, rare-steak-and-red-wine dinners with the one I love, the girl with whom I feel I'm sharing blood.

There are dazzling porcelain dildos for sale, a perfect example of the insouciant extravagance leatherfolk cherish. "Don't these break?" I ask the vendor. "Not when you're fucking," she replies, insouciantly. A male instructor with very strong arms at the hands-on flogging workshop wears a gray leather shirt of a buttery softness so exquisite I could touch it all day, whether I wanted to do S/M with him or not. Jo Arnone, a calm, scary woman who co-founded New York's first lesbian S/M organization with the writer Dorothy Allison, wears an equally supple and touchable hunting shirt of brown leather, so wonderful to feel that it belies the big whip in her hand.

Where is all this beauty coming from? At the moment, decked out in a cute military pin and a *Road Warrior*-macho sort of vest that might make me appear as the nasty young overseer in an intergalactic mining colony, I don't know, but I do know that S/M has opened up the world of beauty to me. I have never been so much in love, never felt so much possibility in my life as I do right now. All is juicy and green, and everything seems within my grasp, including soul-connection of an extent that humbles me. If anyone else has glimpsed these hated parts of myself, they have not loved them. Sara Transom does. She's not repelled by the most repellent things within my soul, but entranced by them. Shockingly and for no good reason I can figure out, she loves me.

"My pit bull!" Sara says, laughing, running to me and kissing me. She loves the part of me that rips things up, the part that snarls and mangles. Without the part of me that's terrifying, she wouldn't have me. "My beautiful pit bull!" As we stand and look at a sort of museum exhibit in the Marketplace called the Steel Bondage Exploratorium, love wells up from the two-hundred-year-old slave irons and prison fetters. At least it seems to. In bed, we read each other Swinburne:

> "If you were Queen of Pleasure
> And I were King of Pain,
> We'd hunt down Love together,
> Pluck out his flying-feather,
> And teach his foot a measure,
> And find his mouth a rein.
> If you were Queen of Pleasure,
> And I were King of Pain."

Whether it comes from the fetters or not, there's certainly love between us. Once, when Sara realizes she's hurt me (entirely apart from S/M), she takes me to a quiet bar and spends the evening holding my hand in both of hers. "You looked so sad. I never want to make you look that way again," she says, "never," and she doesn't take her eyes away from me, but keeps looking at me, sadly and with warmth. That night still counts as one of my most genuine memories of love. Feeling Sara's hands grip me tightly, looking at her open, hot face, I know we are connected, that in spite of all the bars on our cells and the glittering razor wire, we've come close together.

But. But. How can I begin to say how horrible it was, what a horror there was near the core of our love? How can I write about something precious and filthy at once?

ℛ

"Try to avoid wraparound," the beautiful man in an exquisite gray leather shirt is telling us. "That's when the edge will wrap around the body, hitting some of those bony problem areas." If despite your best efforts, the whip wraps, "acknowledge it. I usually say something like 'That probably hurt you, didn't it?'" His tone has turned tender, even solicitous. "Let me hurt you in some other way instead."

It's early and I've had only one cup of coffee, but I'm taking notes carefully. This is one of the things I really need to learn.

This is me writing, at my first flagellation workshop. I wrote the above for a never-finished article for the *Village Voice* about the 1994 Celebration. I really did feel that earnest about learning how to use huge heavy whips without harming anyone. Those who have never attempted it usually don't understand that sadism (in the topsy-turvy world of S/M, if nowhere else) involves, peculiarly but profoundly, *an attempt to be good.* Tops in S/M land don't do what they do simply for the joy of punishing, but also for the joy of *punishing without hurting, being sadistic without killing,* and, you might say, *looking like an abuser without being one.*

My hand starts to cramp up from excessive note-taking, but I keep writing conscientiously. I have never been so responsible (or in a way, so prim). As "the beautiful man" in gray informs us that he likes to do "a lot of coaching and getting feedback" with the men he flogs, I note happily to myself that I have abandoned most of the things I like to do in S/M—and in just plain sex—so I can concentrate on the three activities Sara's fond of. (Unfortunately, all but one of the three leave me cold or repelled, but I do them anyway.) Sara's the bottom, so her desires matter more than mine. If I'm a pit bull, after all, I can't be permitted to do *everything* I might enjoy.

Making love with her, I devote the greater part of my mind to protecting my lover from my fiercest desires. I *am* a superhero—rational beyond human capacity during sex, endlessly tabulating safety and consent in my head, like an adding machine that will not die. Thinking of our lately drab, tense lovemaking, I begin to wonder why I feel so deprived.

But I damp these thoughts down hastily. Thankfully, fantasy matters more in S/M than reality, and in the fantasy, I am Sara's tyrant, and she is my earth, my colonies, my deaf-mute wife. Let everyone who questions this fantasy observe my eagle pin, the black whip I've just bought, and Sara's whispered suggestion that I am her grizzled rapist. I am beyond frustration, beyond need. That's what being Master means.

Jo Arnone has joined the Beautiful Gray Man at the front of the flogging workshop, and the two of them proceed to whip their sacred victims to a background of ominous classical music (which turns out to be the theme from *Bram Stoker's Dracula*.) Like me, Jo and the Gray Man like looking evil. The tops' chiseled faces are gleeful as they contemplate their victims' naked backs ("The first thing I always do is examine the skin," Jo informs us, fingering her partner like a piece of chicken breast). Then Jo and Mr. Gray whale away at their people, beaming. I know this enormous pleasure, and I've shared it. It is the glee of being unpleasant, showing people the most noxious part of yourself and having them like it, breaking rules to loud and public acclaim—like a fantasy of farting and having everyone enjoy the wicked winds you void. It is the glee that all tops feel inside the leather wonderland, and perhaps the reason they put up with a level of responsibility that would drive lesser humans mad.

Jo merrily proceeds to give a lesson on the different types of whips, explaining their origins in farming. "Most of these whips were never intended to hurt the animal," she chuckles, "unlike the way we use them." Farm animals have much thicker hides than human beings do. Still, Jo laughs, "I have never ridden a horse with a crop—I think that's cruel." The audience titters. A woman in the front row cackles, "Right on, Jo! Leashes are for people, not for dogs."

Like so many of us in this room, Jo clearly enjoys showing off her desire to hurt. "Personally, I find belts boring, so I try to use the most painful one possible. . . . The cat-o'-nine-tails is the only whip developed exclusively for human torment. Thus, it is my personal favorite. . . . Forty lashes in the good old days could be a death sentence, they would take cords of hemp and tie pieces of glass, pieces of wire, onto the tails, dip them in vinegar and salt and molten lead. It was kind of neat." She is more charismatic and charming than these sentences might make her seem. "Thank you so much!" she murmurs warmly to a gay male bottom as she strikes him. (His response to the blow, if not to the expression of gratitude, is "Ooomph! Good morning, America!") In the four or five S/M workshops I see her give over a period of several years, Jo is always warmhearted, always radiantly grateful to her bottoms, a mysterious combination of hamming and humble.

Like many sadists, Arnone is also passionately and inordinately fond of words. "*Taw* or *tawse* means 'to further use or prepare for manipulation,'" she crows, holding up the whip named after the word, once used extensively in the Scottish public school system. "It's an archaic word in Scotch dialect! It also means 'to beat,'" she tells us fondly. I get the idea that Jo, like me, is capable of being aroused by the thesaurus entries for *Punishment, Subjugation* ("tamed, broken to harness . . . led by the nose, dominated, browbeaten . . . treated like dirt under one's feet"), and *Retaliation*. About the tawse, she speaks a line that could come from a splendid country song: "It's the most brutal thing I've ever seen, and it made me want to go to Scotland."

Me, I don't mind at all hearing about the unfortunate youngsters of Scotland—their predicament, in 1994, sounds pretty sexy to me—but I do feel a shiver of cognitive dissonance whenever Jo mentions political tortures in the same breath as the "safe, sane, and consensual" S/M that I so righteously practice. When she says "It was kind of neat" about the cat-o'-nine-tails that were used to execute people two hundred years ago, I write *"Sick"* in my notes. Then I'm mortified at myself. I'm a sanctified S/M convert, and I know that attitudes are never sick—only actions are. How'd this impiety get in my head?

Then Jo says, sadly, about the cat-o'-nine-tails, "It was really brutal, and we can't do this anymore." She pauses. "Anybody who knows me knows why I can't use these anymore, even though I used to like it."

If you listen to tops talk long enough, you'll come to understand that for them, S/M is, among other things, a Platonic investigation into restraint and self-knowledge. Tops—like Jo at this moment, scrupulously informing us about her imperfections—are perpetually examining the content of their character, taking a reckoning of the good and evil in themselves, trying to ascertain what distinguishes them from the abusers they try hard to resemble. "Don't you hope I'm an ethical and compassionate human being?" one character asks another in a Pat Califia porn story. "Aren't you glad you're too big to be stuffed in the trash compactor?" The joke about putting the bottom in the compactor makes the top's self-investigation sexy: "Am I bad or I am good?" is the recurrent, defining question for consensual sadists, and the teasing threat-and-promise of that very question is the lure they use to get masochists into bed. The erotic appeal of S/M is in the *appearance* of evil, the *threat* of evil, but the reason people join the S/M lifestyle is S/M culture's assurance that the top will stay "good." As Califia's character Reid reflects after teasing her partner with this tantalizing contradiction, "The restraint she had to place on her own sadism had to be stronger than any chain that locked somebody else to her bed."

Tops think about responsibility about as frequently as conservative Christians do, and their obsessive self-questioning about sin and justification is, if anything, more intense. Conservative Christians are preoccupied with the image of Christ dying for them, but sadists in the leather world are confronted on a daily basis with live human beings bleeding and suffering for *them*. Perhaps it's natural that the feelings that get stirred up in both cases are similar. Am I worthy of this person's pain? Am I loving and safe enough to deserve this person's gift? Can I make my lover's suffering meaningful?

Can I, too, imitate Christ by making my partner's pain pleasurable, turning water into wine? Can I, too, turn torture into an Ascension? Can we redeem each other?

Bottoms sometimes speak of tops as their gods, but when tops speak of holy presences among the whips and chains, they are much more likely to be talking about the divinity of the masochist. "Without them, I am *nothing*," Jo Arnone tells the audience at another flogging workshop. Califia's character Reid is filled with "awe" by her partner's ability to come from being tortured with an electric wand. "Masochists were so amazing," she thinks to herself. "They took her need to hurt and made it beautiful."

In another Califia porn story, "The Calyx of Isis," one of seven topwomen tells their victim, "The light from the stained-glass window is falling on your body. . . . It falls in patterns of pure color. You are elevated there for our adoration. The scapegoat, the sacred victim. In you we find forgiveness, resurrection."

When Sara Transom lies across my lap, waiting for the ritual we think will expiate us both, I feel like someone who has been offered the classic Christian second chance. I understand, doubling my belt in my hands, that it's been hard for me to love because love has been mixed with torture in my family—not absent, but just always mixed with the taut and the terrifying. "All my tenderness," I write, "was secreted behind a brutality I was afraid to touch."

I think that by training the belt on Sara, I will finally come close to love, and for a time it works.

꘠

In one of the ecstasies of self-awareness that perpetually get S/M folks high, I tell Sara that S/M, for me, is a lot about loving those who have harmed you. (Bringing a rolled-up belt with you is essential.) "For me," she responds, "it's about being loved by them."

There has to be a strange metaphysic at work in a discipline that makes you think you can figure out how to love one person by beating up another. But then, S/M is the most metaphysical (and, certainly, the most intellectual) of all sexual practices—the one that inspired its most famous practitioner to write a book called *Philosophy in the Bed-room* in which sentences like "Her ass is all yours. Suck it for her while my tongue licks her cunt" are combined with sentences like "Had man been formed wholly good, man should never be able to do evil, and only then would the work be worthy of a god. To allow man to choose was to tempt him; and God's infinite powers very well advised him of what would be the result."

In her brilliantly erudite introduction to *her* first book of porn, *Macho Sluts,* Pat Califia goes Sade one better, explicitly comparing sadomasochism to Plato. Speaking of readers who are horrified by the things she finds erotic, Califia asks, "Do these people hate me, do they want sado-masochists to cease to exist, because of a different notion about what constitutes the good and the beautiful?"

What constitutes the good and the beautiful—and how you can integrate the good and the beautiful into your life—are two of the S/M world's most driving questions. But the Platonic inquiry with which S/M is even more concerned is about the relation between reality and "simu-lacra," or as Plato preferred to think of it, between the world of appearances and the world of the spirit. Plato called the spirit real and the world of material reality a false and inferior "copy," and in their own way, S/M activists do the same. But what is being endlessly "copied" and transmuted in S/M land is violence, which is why S/M, unlike Plato, overtly privileges the fake over the real. Fake violence is indisputably "better," at least ethically.

Deep down, though, sadomasochists are uneasily uncertain about what the relationship between "real" and "copied" violence really is, and how the two things should or shouldn't be brought together in their practice. The highly charged and contradictory relationship between violence in the world and violence in one's soul is itself the beating heart of S/M, the reason S/M porn is full of braggadocio to the effect that the sexual coercion between bottoms and tops is "real," while S/M cultural and political writing is simultaneously full of assurances that it is fake.

"Violence, rape, and incest are horribly common in this country," Barry Douglas, the former chairman of Gay Male S/M Activists, announces at a press conference during the Leather Celebration. "One of the reasons for conferences like this is to distinguish between those violent people and human freedom."

But what, in fact, *is* the difference between "those violent people" and human freedom?

The basic erotic question in S/M—can the top simultaneously release her violent impulses and control them?—is essentially a variant of well-known theological questions about free will and human ethics. Why would we have all these impulses, if they were intrinsically evil? Is the human will sufficiently powerful that we can each control them if we want to? Who is to blame for the imperfection of our control? It's no accident that Sade and other sadomasochists are markedly obsessed with the issue of why a good God would create human beings with the ability to sin against each other as horrifically as they do. Contrary to their public persona, S/M people are not defenders of sin, but people horrified by sin—especially, painfully, and acutely horrified.

"I don't believe in an omnipotent, omniscient God," Califia writes in *Macho Sluts,* "because that would make the world a truly horrible place, beyond human redemption." Sade dedicates *Justine* "to my lady friend, Constance" who alone will understand that the purpose of his novel, in which an innocent woman is repeatedly raped and hurt, is to make people "love" the virtuous heroine and detest her assailants. (Andrea Dworkin's novel, *Mercy,* whose plot is almost identical, was written with a similar purpose.) With only half his tongue in his cheek, and more anger for God's cruelty than is usually acknowledged, Sade expresses the hope that Constance will say after reading it, "Oh, how much these pictures of crime make me proud to love virtue! How sublime she is in her tears!" "Oh, Constance," Sade ends his dedication, "let but these words drop from your lips, and my labors are crowned!"

Like Christian rightists, S/M people are obsessed with the question of "What is to be done" about sin—or as S/M people generally prefer to call it, violence. Like the Christian right, when they ask this question, they don't mean "How do we end violence today in the world?" but "What do we do with the violence we have ourselves experienced, and how do we relate this violence to love [or, as the Christians would put it, to Love]?"

S/M's method of redemption is quite close to Christianity's, although a bit more self-aware. The amazingly idealist notion that has won S/M so many converts in our time is that difficult things in the "real" world can be redeemed by their simulacra inside the "fake" world of sexuality. (The woman who wears a black hankie in her right pocket to celebrate her own triumph over undesired pain is not too different from the churchgoer who kneels each week before a stylized image of a Roman torture device. By bearing the cross as a symbol, we think we can bear the real crosses in our lives. Something that neither S/M people nor Christian rightists ever say is that in reality, violence, torture, and agony *cannot be borne,* almost by definition. And almost by definition, they cannot be redeemed.)

~

"I want to relate an experience that my partner had in playing with fire with someone," Bear Thunder Fire tells us at the "Ready? . . . Flame . . . Fire! Temperature Torture" panel later that afternoon. "We'd wiped her down [to clean her up after a previous scene] with alcohol, which we'd thought had dried off. Then we started on her with the torch. But what happened was the alcohol had run down her sides, and she caught. The carpet was a polyester blend. The next room had wool carpeting, so instead of diving for the floor, she dove for the next room."

Bear continues: "So when you play with fire, you need to ask yourself, Do I really want to spend the next two weeks taking care of someone if something happens? Make sure that, whoever you play with, you really like. We had to nurse and feed this woman for three days." The seventy of us leatherfolk cramped into a tiny Hyatt meeting room take notes assiduously. This highly technical workshop also covers hurting people with jalapeños, Tabasco, and Vicks VapoRub, and though these are all less damaging than fire, they're meant to evoke the agonies of skin burn just the same.

But Bear Thunder Fire's recommendations for playing with fire don't sound all that sexy, even to my deliriously sadist self of 1994. "You want to have things like a fire extinguisher and a wet towel on hand," she lectures us. "Whether you're experienced or not, I strongly suggest having several people around when you do this kind of scene. Don't ever take anything for granted, because bad things can happen! Make sure what you're playing on is not a material that will catch. Lay cotton over a linoleum floor. Have Silverdine available, which is what you put immediately onto a burned area. And you have to be aware of where someone's hair is. Have them wear a ban- dana—I don't care if it doesn't look pretty, fashion can wait at the dungeon door."

Bear concludes: "Fire is probably one of the cruelest monsters that I've gotten to play with. Even though they put me on a panel, I don't call myself an expert, because to me an expert is someone who can have total control of something, and you can't have that with fire."

☞

Although people who play with fire in S/M (sometimes) really do get burned, all consensual sadomasochism nonetheless takes place in quotes, as though it were a scene on stage. And in fact, setting someone on fire with a first-aid kit and fire extinguisher nearby is something that might conceivably happen in a performance piece. Most S/M fire-players keep the fire lit for only a few seconds, with no intention of burning the person—making the eroticism, for both parties, entirely a matter of the mind. Though S/M isn't wholly unreal, it depends heavily on the imagination, and leatherfolk exalt it for that: the incantatory ecstasy of S/M sex is about the ironic, symbolic, and "performative" continually triumphing over and transcending the poor, shoddy unchangeables of history and experience. Does abuse hurt? Then make it not hurt in your mind!

It's no accident that S/M political activists have jauntily adopted the language of postmodern literary criticism, decrying "real gender" and insisting that acts like whipping have *no* inherent meaning. Like the lit critics, leatherfolk worship Foucault without really remembering what he said—that genuine liberation was much harder to achieve than any of us imagine. For all their hatred of universal concepts, fundamentally both S/M and postmodern lit crit are bastard heirs of Platonism, ways of exalting ideas over the flesh.

"With some bottoms, it is actually a mystical experience," Jo Arnone tells us at the flogging workshop. "There is nothing sexual about it. We are on a higher plane."

The Gray Man drones on and on about the correct way to clean various kinds of whips (Mediquik, Betadine, rubbing alcohol, or Simple Green) and the need to "recondition" the whips afterward with Hubbard's Shoe Grease or Murphy's Oil. He has a sweet sort of boring-schoolteacher quality to him, which also came through when he was telling how to flick the whip ergonomically and without stimulating your bottom's "abuse issues."

But the man he's been beating, Winn Miller, is even more boring when *he* begins to lecture us: "When I'm being whipped I see things in color. I transport all my feelings into colors. At all of the chakras, I get the ROY-G-BIV spectrum. It's sort of like a melting into yourself. My visualization of the flogging is that it's a caress, it's lovemaking. You can have this out-of-body experience and this light show." Tops are rather boringly focused on other people, I think confusedly, reviewing my list of instructions for preparing anti-bacterial solutions for cleaning flails and putting people in bondage without putting any stress on their joints. But bottoms, I am slowly realizing, seem to be even more boringly focused on themselves. "I just love it when I sit at my desk in my Giorgio Armani suit and my secretary comes in, and I lean back and say, 'Mmm,'" Wynn apprises us, "and my secretary says, 'Oh, what were *you* doing last night?'"

He continues: "It is better than any drug. I have afterglow. There are some moments when I actually leave my body. Where I'm looking down from above and seeing the guy beating me, and I'm not in my body. There is nothing like that!"

My fantasy life flourishes when I come into S/M, but it becomes my major concern when I start going out with Sara, two years later. Never have I spent so much time spinning elaborate sexual tales and sharing them with another intelligence. We send each other passionate e-mail several times a day about the things we'd like to do with each other. My colleagues at work are titillated and, very probably, annoyed by my endless, loud sexual phone calls in my cubicle.

Finally, I am what I dreamed of being at sixteen—a full-blown pervert! A genuine nasty girl! I dress with care each morning, excited about everything from the angle of my hair to the freewheeling macho-ness of my shiny combat boots. On my dresser, I compile a collection of hair-brushes, markers, and shoehorns to be used in penetration. I feel so ready for the voluptuousness that awaits me.

I am beguiled beyond belief by Sara Transom, who sits with me on our first date drinking tea and handing me buttered crumpets as we discuss retaliation, sweet, sweet forgiveness, and the feeling of wooden paddles on a bare red butt. Sara is warmer than anyone I've ever dated, and her face is more open, more eager to encounter—something. Sweetness, innocence, and likeableness emanate from that handsome teenage boy profile. I've done S/M before, but never with anyone so searching and self-aware. The night of our formal, second date, we stay up all night sampling the power of my right and left hands and screwing. And also talking about the connection we are making through my drumming hands. It's one of the most romantic evenings of my life.

❧

The next day, I stagger into work at three P.M. and give everyone briefings on my extraordinarily physical, highly manual evening, like Winn Miller. I feel like something I never feel like half as much as I want to: a sexual creature. I am one, I am one, I am one! We stayed up all night doing it, and in an utterly radical way, too! A way that would upset people! Are you blushing yet? Dorothy Allison has an essay in an S/M anthology in which she makes a similarly inordinate, unnecessarily emphatic and defiant protestation: "Fucking, fucking, fucking. I call this fucking. . . . I am angry all the time lately, and being angry makes me horny . . . makes me want to shock strangers and surprise the girls who ask me, please, out for coffee and to talk. I don't want to talk . . . I am doing it as much as I can, as fast as I can. This holy act . . . I am licking their necks on Market Street, fisting them in the second-floor bathroom at Amelia's, in a booth under a dim wall lamp at The Box . . . I have ripped open their jeans at the Powerhouse, put my heel between their legs at the Broadway Cafe, opened their shirts all the way down at Just Desserts, and pushed seedless grapes into their panties at the Patio Cafe. The holy act of sex . . . I am doing it, boys and girls, I am doing it, doing it all the time."

I've always worshipped sex, like Allison, and like Allison, too, I suspect, felt guilty for not having enough. I have spent my life afraid of being insufficiently sexual—why?—and literally feeling I have sinned against a godhead when I haven't been sexual, intoxicated, fevered, ecstatic enough. As Pentecostal theologian Charles G. Finney writes: "Christians are as guilty for not being filled with the Holy Spirit as sinners are for not repenting. They are even more so, for as they have more light, they are so much the more guilty." I have believed as much all my life, and hated myself for not being so filled. "Abstinence sows sand all over the ruddy limbs and flaming hair," Blake wrote, and I felt like a creature of sand. All the words emanating from the old Dionysiac worship—*ecstasy, enthusiasm, orgies, rapture*—refer to the god being in you, or you being taken out of yourself by the god. All my life I have wanted this personal relationship with the Intoxicating Saviour, the god who comes bringing fire.

My new lover has ripped jeans and an endless desire to be thrown against the wall. I have snagged the brass ring, finally proved myself. Sara really thinks I'm sexy! None of my other lovers has found me quite this sexy, or if they have, I haven't been able to hear it. Like a caricature of a rich, powerful straight man, I take Sara out for oysters, hunks of red meat, and champagne, all on me. She has become my lady, or my child. For my birthday, she buys me a box of paternal and masculine items that give me a little thrill in the solar plexus: an ancient, handsome pocketknife, poker chips, a leather whiskey flask, the pin with the eagle on it (a symbol loved both by "Love it or leave it" types and fascists), old maps of the world, a key with many-digited numbers on it like the numbers on Jews' arms. (Nazi fantasies hover at the edge of consciousness for many, many fantasizers, even Jews like me.)

Fantasy and reality keep crossing for us. In the bloom of our love, there seems to be no difference between them. On one of our early expensive-restaurant dates, I tell her I'd like her to dress differently from now on. She does. It's sexy to interact with her as though she were required to please me, but secretly, and very deep down, part of me believes it's all real. Part of me believes I do control her, and that now I really will get everything I want. Somewhere, I believe that because I am in love with a masochist, I have entered the Garden of Eden.

℞

Sex has always terrified me. I have hardly ever said so. Like Dorothy Allison, I get horny when I get angry. I also get angry when I get horny. But the connection between my sex and my rage terrifies me. Embarked on this bold voyage of sex with Sara, I have never really understood why people find sexual sensations *pleasurable*. I find arousal mostly frightening and torturous. Yet I keep seeking it out—because of biology? Because I can only dream there's something more? Because I think that if I only keep doing this frightening, maddening thing I can control it? Because I feel sex is my job and I'm supposed to do it?

Until my midtwenties, I let myself be literally frustrated by sex. The sensations before orgasm were unbearable, and on some not very conscious level, I decided not to bear them. I began shutting down in the very days when I, a high school Greek and Latin student, literally worshipped Dionysus and was known among my friends for boisterously requesting the god on every picnic and park outing to take me over. Like Christ (who took on very many of his attributes), Dionysus is the god of getting out of prison, the god of the Door, the Spirit, and the Life. But worshipping getting out of prison and worshipping the prison can come to be equated. "Even now he is near and sees what I undergo," the bacchic Stranger tells Pentheus, the king who is binding him down, in Euripides' *Bacchae*. Dionysus is more than near; he is actually incarnated in the shackled Stranger. It is the same with Christ, who became human so that he could know what it was like to feel human torments. Those who worship him venerate him

137

for his confinement and torture as much as for any release that he brings. In Christianity, in fact, the two cannot be separated.

In the worship of Dionysus they cannot be separated, either. The god of release is famous for being jailed, famous for being hurt and put at risk. If he is the only one of the Olympians to be so imperiled, he is also the only one who was born of a human mother; he was snatched up by Zeus and saved when Semele, his pregnant mother, was incinerated because Zeus had sworn to give her whatever she wanted and she'd insisted that he appear to her in his divine form, as a bolt of lightning. In *The Bacchae,* Dionysus and his followers are humiliated, threatened, chained. His divinity is *about* risk, oppression, and confinement as much as it is about liberation. If he were not so chained, he would not instill violence in his followers. And if he were not so humiliated, he would not instill madness in them.

In S/M, too, explosion and restraint come down to pretty much the same thing. An erotic picture that encapsulates the deliciousness of S/M for me at this time in my life is a photo of a beautiful young Latino man naked among dewy red and yellow flowers. His erection is enormous. He is bound tightly in many white ropes, and his big pink erection is bound more tightly and more painfully than any other part of him.

❧

Part of me doesn't think sex has to be like this. I have had hints—tender but gorgeous feelings, like those of sweet lips around my nipples, early autoerotic moments that were gentle, sunny, and warm, the one time I had sex on hashish, the essential friendliness of touching the other's body, feeling in the other's human trunk a basic goodness that I want to second.

Leather is not about this, but in 1994 I do not yet know why. I know that invoking my terror will somehow get me through my terror. In the myth, holding up Medusa's head, with its terrifying snakes for hair, gives you power over things that terrify; flaunting the monster's head as obnoxiously as you can gives you power over monsters. Invoking my own fear of sex makes me come. Approaching a woman with a whip in my hands, as Nietzsche advised, makes approaching a woman tolerable for me. Little else does.

Holding a vibrator to my own genitals as I slap Sara's with a tiny "cunt whip" made of soft short tails, I am not sure whether the violence takes care of my fears about the sex, or the sex is taking care of my fears about violence. I know the word *apotropaic* (warding off), which was used of people holding up the Medusa's head to banish this or that terror. And I know I am warding off something. But I am not sure whether I am warding off sex or violence. I do know that I love the poster that Pat Califia gave a friend of mine, which said NO CUTENESS SHOULD GO UNPUNISHED. I feel the same way. If I explicitly punish beauty, it will be safe to welcome beauty in my life.

A month or so into our relationship, I begin feeling confused about what sex is, and whether there is really any of it in my life. We spend most of our time together talking about sex (that is, about S/M). We develop an elaborate idea for an S/M restaurant years before La Nouvelle Justine opens in New York with lots of beef and pork on the menu and waiters who will whip you, for a price. And we even spend a lot of time "doing" S/M—that is to say, I strike Sara with a belt or a whip, and then, if she seems to want me to, I get her off. I am confused about why it all feels so unfulfilling.

Sara doesn't like to touch *me*—especially not in any way that might make me have an orgasm. For a long, long time, we speak of this as though it were a natural consequence of our doing S/M. In fact, most S/M scenes have no genital contact in them, and those that do rarely have much genital contact *for the top*. If there is an orgasm in an actual S/M scene, it is much more likely to be the bottom's. Pat Califia complains about this problem in her wonderfully titled essay "Mr. Benson Doesn't Live Here Anymore": "The community expectation seems to be that 'real tops' don't need to come." S/M, after all, is about one partner losing control, and the other holding tight to it. Sara doesn't mind touching my breasts, but she's surprised and not a little offended when I say I'm frustrated because that's all she ever does. I mean, she has limits after all! Why don't I want her to honor them?

I'm not sure exactly why my lover doesn't like her partner to come. But those are her limits, and I do honor them. S/M is, more than anything, about honoring the bottom's limits. Whatever threat my genitals are to her, they are a threat greater than whips and rolled-up belts. My arousal scares her more than being gagged, tied up, and beaten with a hairbrush. So I don't make her go through it. S/M is, after all, about compassion, and about consent—about sparing people pain that they don't choose.

Soon enough, she stops wanting me to touch *her* genitals, either. Our sexuality becomes completely a matter of painful blows, and fantasies. I don't understand what I'm doing, coming home night after night to turn on a rage that is becoming increasingly real and thrash someone I love in a way that feels increasingly unconsenting for *me*. I've found one of the loves of my life, and the only way that I can touch her is with variously stinging bits of leather.

~

The only way for me to go out of control is to hit her in a way she doesn't want. But I don't do that. The closest I come is to engage in scenes sometimes when I'm angry, which you're not supposed to do. But my control over myself is iron, and I never blow. (In my head, late at night, I'm starting to imagine that as freedom.) My responsibilities as a top are rather confounding; I'm supposed to excite the bottom by the prospect of my going out of control. But never do it. I'm supposed to excite myself by the image of myself as an abuser—but never become one.

I think S/M is teaching me morality, and in a way it is. I certainly never thought so much about compassion as I do now, when I have regular permission to hurt someone. Seeing yourself as a non-victim makes it hard to assume that other people are always to blame, so to this extent, the practice of sadism is vastly improving my character. Seeing yourself as an official dominant makes it hard to assume that you're entitled to do anything you want because of what you have endured—the classic "victim attitude." It makes me understand, in a way, the Promise Keepers' concept of "servant leadership," which is the idea that men, if they really, *really* take on the task of "leading" their family, actually become its most abject servants. It makes me understand a great deal about men in general, actually, and the habitual bitterness in their lives; how awful it is to feel always dominant, always responsible, always to blame.

In a workshop at the Celebration on domestic violence in the S/M community, I raise my hand and ask a question that, years later, still shocks me. "With my girlfriend, I've been doing scenes with her sometimes when I've been angry, and I'm a little worried about it." In a way, the question is disingenuous; I'm not really *that* worried, because I know I have bound my violence tighter than Satan. I'm asking the question because part of me *wants* to see myself as truly capable of going out of control with Sara; truly capable of getting what I need. It's a nice image: slamming her across the teeth, with no restraint.

I feel so deprived, frustrated, and repressed by now that that sounds good to me. I feel powerless with the Transom girl, and on some level even my 1994 self, caught up in the bliss of make-believe, knows that *that* feeling, not power, is the root of all real violence. Dominance is its own punishment because no control is complete; dominators are always ruled by their fear of the unmasterable, even if the least masterable thing of all turns out to be themselves. What upsets me today, remembering this time, is knowing that I probably really was in danger of becoming the abuser that S/M is an ongoing effort to cage.

The S/M anti-violence activists at the workshop give me good tribal advice. "Don't play from anger at all," they tell me. "When you're doing S/M, avoid psychological hot spots!" But S/M is almost exclusively *about* psychological hot spots. People do it because they see it as a way to transcend past rage and helplessness, to convert the dross of one's life into gold. (Why are they surprised when the dross keeps coming back in one form or another?)

ß

Afterward I go home and "confess" to Sara that I've done scenes with her while I was angry and that the domestic-violence-workshop folks confirmed my thought that this was bad. Sara simply adds this to my mammoth list of wrongs, which largely consists of strapping her the wrong way, sometimes literally on the wrong cheek, with the wrong rhythm, not hard enough, not hard enough to give her an endorphin rush, not imaginatively enough, too sexually, not sexually enough, and simply not boldly enough, and sometimes *just not strapping her enough* but just asking her what she thinks about various scenarios, when I should be hitting her!

ß

In a dream, Sara and I are rowing through an ocean of pastry cream. We stop and feed each other the ocean cream and berries and chocolate bits of the hull. The air itself turns into colorless eau-de-vie, and we pour it into each other's mouths as our tongues go inside, too, sliding oblong fruit, and I am with my love without a barrier.

🎗

This will never happen. S/M is a mystical practice that tries to get to this place by never getting there, like the monks who ate dung to see God. I became a sex radical because I thought it would open me up to this bit of heaven, save me for it, make it safe for me.

Instead, what I have are the bars: my chest of torture devices (including an item that would hurt anyone who dared to make love to me by giving them electric shocks); all sorts of restraints; a leash; tight, cold handcuffs; a beautiful whip that could slice open someone's back; a police truncheon; nasty little straps; and something called a pigslapper.

Truth is, pleasure, trust, and love are themselves threatening to me, unless they are buffered by some sort of police action. Sex and love must have their feathers plucked out before I'll have them, as in Swinburne's poem; they have to have their feet tied down, their mouths reined, their wings shot to nothing if I'm going to let them in my company.

🎗

I am calling off my guards and taking off my reins. I am giving away my stun gun. I don't want to make this tawdry redemptive trade-off anymore, even though in some ways it did open me to that beautiful place. S/M is tantalizing, in the original sense of the man condemned to have beautiful banquets put before him that he was never allowed to eat. S/M brings people closer to love and sex, but only by keeping them at endless arm's length; it opens the door, perhaps, by showing it is not a door.

𝒻ℴ

Coming out into S/M, I felt I had been born again in an even more redemptive sense than when I came out as gay. Coming out as gay gave me a convenient way to frame my sense of powerlessness and my sense of being hated; coming out into S/M gave me an even more comprehensive way to turn all of my negative experiences into love.

I don't mean to belittle that effort. There is a sweetness and, indeed, an innocence to S/M that I will always respect. Despite what it says about itself, S/M is not sex on the edge of danger, but sex hemmed in with safety. Leather jackets were originally adopted by motorcyclists because they protect the body from blows; they became the symbol of sadomasochism for the same reason. You can't turn all of your negative experiences into love, though it is sweet to try. But I'll be born again no more. The protection of S/M is no protection; being saved, by this mystery or any other, will not save me.

I don't feel like a sex radical now, but like a fleer from sex. I remember all the times I tried to insert sex into my conversations, into my politics, into my life as much as possible. Into my writing, into my workplace, even into my home decorating (a giant S/M photo to entertain my guests over dinner: a man with a big, pretty erection, getting stepped on). I loved being at the *Village Voice,* where you could rant about sex all day long in the course of your regular work, and put up lesbian agitprop posters full of messages like "And then my tongue between her thighs . . . I would tease her nipples . . . lay her on her back . . ." These endless invocations had the quality of a protestation. As though I had a sexual inquisitor after me, I swore up and down every day and in every possible way, *sex is really in my life, it's really in my life, it's really in my life!*

It wasn't—at least, not to the extent of being able to feel it—*really feel it*—without abject fear.

One of the really noble, even humanist things about S/M is that it is an effort to feel. To feel even as you feel the terror, *to feel something,* not to close off. It's as though Sara Transom and I had bravely put spacesuits on to wander through a perilous alien garden. I've had to leave it only because it did not let me feel enough.

Beyond redemption is another garden.

6

The Flower Bed

"This is, and thou art," Ursula Le Guin writes in one of her most hopeful passages, in a book about the end of the world. "There is no safety, and there is no end." So begins my anti-redemption. Peculiarly, life is more fun when you understand that you can't transcend anything. In the sad, fun time after transcendence leaves my life, one of the first things that changes is my attitude toward femininity.

I take an aerobics class with lots of straight women, and I don't hate them. I don't hate myself, either, not even when I mambo, shake, and flounce during the Aerobic Dance portion. The picture of not hating myself shaking like a girl is so new for me it feels almost like rebirth. "You know, when you cross the paths of women, you change," the warm and earnest speaker tells us at the very next Christian right event I hit. Strangely, I feel all warm inside, as though I were back at the women's center at Yale, not surrounded by Christian women of all ages in a beautiful womblike church. Grace 'N Vessels holds its services in one of those trailer-ish, prefabricated buildings chosen by more and more right-wing churches in these "End Times" days, but this one is actually incredibly lovely, with a deep blue carpet on the floors and on the wall behind the altar. The undulant design makes you feel as though you're on a ship, or maybe in a cradle.

I've felt rocked to an odd sort of peace ever since I stepped inside and was greeted with strawberries, danish and coffee, and a *kaffeeklatsch* of Christian women that reminds me uncannily of my mother's cronies in Great Neck. When I first saw the ad for this gathering in *Charisma,* I thought it would be hideous. "We invite you to experience Total Woman Ministries . . . A ministry designed to equip women: spirit, body & soul," the notice coaxed, showing before-and-after photos of women whose skin, clothes, and hair had been restyled for the Lord.

The text said that Christian attendees would "witness" "dramatic makeovers done by our team of professionals. You'll learn about national trends in hair and fashion for 1996 in our lively forum designed to give women a greater level of effectiveness as ambassadors of Jesus Christ." The photos showed three sad women without makeup transformed into gleaming zombies for Phyllis Schlafly. In the "before" pictures the women looked strong, intelligent, and real. "After," they'd turned into mindless animals. Their smiles, underneath elaborate hairdos and facepaint, were frighteningly vacuous. They appeared to be blissed out and full of rage at once.

"Your ministry delightfully transformed our women and brought a heightened understanding to the beauty of holiness," the ad went on—a testimonial from a local pastor. Reading it, I was terrified. Transforming myself into a woman has always been the hardest part of my undercover work with the religious right. In fact, I'm sure that one reason I'm a lesbian is because, this way, I don't have to be "a woman" very often. When I prepare for Christian trips, my gradual feminization is the opposite of most conversion experiences; instead of feeling joy in "the clothes of the new man," I feel fear and disgust in them. Mortification as I set a flowered hat on my head, a sense of shame as I paint myself . . .

Becoming this creature that I cannot stand (who *is* she?), "the flower of womanhood," is even more intense and complicated for me than becoming a fascist or gay-hater, identities I've put on in my undercover work with relative ease. For me, looking like a woman is harder than clapping for Pat Buchanan. It feels humiliating to wear clothes like this—and sexual. And somehow abominable. For better or worse, "the flower of womanhood" is an image I have never been able to read as anything but a walking vagina—and I have only been able to read that as negative. The girl who smiles wide, no matter what she's feeling.

But sitting in this soft pew, surrounded by other women, I take a deep breath and try to feel something other than revulsion and hatred. For over a year, I've been trying to feel differently about femininity—other people's and my own. I know that my hatred of femininity goes much deeper than not wanting to wear girl's clothes: my encounters with female members of the Christian right have taught me some uncomfortable lessons about my own hatred of *women*. If there's a single reason I am here at Grace 'N Vessels, it's because I want to stop despising grace and vessels.

"I'm so glad you're here," makeup-evangelist Laura Tucker tells me as she walks through the Danbury, Connecticut, church, shaking women's hands and admiring our outfits. I'm wearing a very nice long flowered dress and a shaped jacket, my newly long and curly hair looks sweet, and I believe her. (I am growing my hair a bit after having kept it close to my head for fifteen years.) Laura and her partner, Gina Kidd, travel the country offering salvation and accessorizing tips—partly in an effort to entice unsaved women into Jesus' arms. ("God has given Total Woman Ministries a unique appeal to women of all walks of life," the ad says. "Consequently, many women who attend would otherwise not hear the gospel.") Most of the women in this room have already received the Spirit, but a strong whiff of the secular and even the commercial blows through the service nonetheless. The altar is bedecked with earrings, hats, and hairsprays—things a previous generation of Pentecostals would never have allowed to touch the holy place.

"I'm loving this," I write in my notebook. Even though what's going on here is the direct antithesis of my favorite ACT UP (and later, Queer Nation) slogan, "We're here, we're queer, we're not going shopping," the paradoxical, camp statement by which Queer Nationals affirmed their militant earnestness. (The chant was followed not long after by the disturbing—and very masculine—"We're here, we're queer / Don't fuck with us, we'll fuck you up.") In contrast, Total Woman's mode of worship—in which women sniff shampoos and try on one another's shoes—can be said to be a form of *anti*-zealotry, or even anti-fundamentalism. These girls are serious about religion,

granted, but they seem to see religion itself as a sort of Ultimate and Glorious Unseriousness, the utter opposite of the
Christian Coalition's worship of tort reform and *Crossfire*.
The hairbrushes, scarves, and other baubles underscore
Gina and Laura's sense of the Holy Spirit as a spirit of love
and frivolity, nurturing and self-nurturing, a feminine light-
heartedness I have always envied and could not take part
in. (I thought it was sacrosanct that I be butch, inflexible,
and grave.) But "In Isaiah it says. 'Behold I am going to do
a new thing!'" Laura interrupts my brooding. "He's saying,
Hey, I want to do a new thing! The old thing wasn't bad,
but now we want to do a new thing!"

The women in the audience laugh appreciatively, fixing
their gaze on the rows of earrings behind her. Unashamedly,
they are as thirsty for new styles as they are for the Living
Water—in fact, new 'dos and clothes seem to be just
another form of Jesus' generous outpouring. Earlier, Gina, a
tall seductress in a shiny red pantsuit, had gone around the
audience asking women if they wanted haircuts. The gals'
responses were a far cry from the Concerned Women for
America—jokes about their own poor grooming, about
Gina's gorgeousness, about what the congregation's female
pastor will say when she sees their hot new looks. This audience is flirtatious as lesbians, salacious as gay men, irrever-
ent as Jewish women. Their sheer joy in the material and the
flighty warms me completely.

When the service starts up, things become a little more
intense. On the stage, Alicia, a twenty-two-year-old with
long hair and a voice like Debbie Gibson, starts singing
about Jesus as though he were a perfect boyfriend: "'Tis
so sweet to trust in Jesus, / Just to take him at his word. /

Just to rest upon his promise. . . ." She cheeps endless variations on this happy theme: song after song about how he's going to come and make her whole again, fulfill all her yearnings, free her from everything that isn't beautiful. By the fifth ballad, women are looking up at God with private smiles. "Jesus, Jesus, how I trust him," Alicia warbles, "How I trust him night and day." Women start to jump and holler, as though they had just remembered a steamy date.

"Oh, she really gets me *on fire!*" Gina says when she takes over from the singer. Gina, who's a professional cosmetologist with a ravenous air, gets the atmosphere even hotter. "He is so madly in love with you," she croons. She goes on to say that God is in love with women who are married, women who are looking for husbands, and—endearingly—women who choose to be "alone." Laura chimes in, playing a *simpatico* Gloria Steinem to Gina's riot grrl: "Open your heart to receive what he would impart to you this day. There's a ministry for you! Whether it's in your home as a wife and mother, or on the job—nobody's gonna be able to tell you which is right for you. *God's* gonna give it to you." Suddenly, we are all holding each other: "Pray for the sister on your left, and for the sister on your right!" Gina booms at us. The woman on whose right I am standing squeezes my hand hard at that, saying, *"Yes! yes! yes!"* I squeeze back. I feel very moved. And I'm also getting turned on. Some of these women are very sexy, either because of their perfervid gestures or their nubile bodies or their friendly grippings of one another's hands. Gina, sounding like the best part of Andrea Dworkin, tells us to pray that God should give ourselves and the other women in the room the things we want and need.

I love her sloppy concern for us, like Andrea's warm sincerity and passion. All around me, women are suddenly making orgasmic cries, praying their own prayers very loud in English, and speaking in tongues (which sounds as though the Spirit were moving through vaginal lips and making them talk). Some of them clutch me hard when Gina invites us to pray that God's goodness be visited on the women sitting next to us. And I do pray, to my surprise. I don't believe in a God who exists independently of our perceptions, but I know I want these women to be nurtured by whatever can nurture them.

We continue to hold each other, and the room is getting a bit hot and airless. *"Yes Lord, yes Lord, whatever you desire!"* and other cries of sorrowful passion all around me. It feels like a cross between a particularly rousing and emotional feminist rally ("STOP THE VIOLENCE! / END THE SILENCE! / WOMEN, UNITE! / WOMEN, UNITE!"), and the lesbian backroom bar I used to go to in New York City, where women poured out God's grace on strangers with some heat—and remarkable goodwill. At the "Labia Lounge," which was the name for women's night at a gay club called the Wonder Bar, everyone who came into the sacred room in back was welcomed and anointed. No one was barred from salvation. Like the Labia Lounge, Grace 'N Vessels extends a promiscuous friendliness that is rarely found outside the church and the gay and lesbian community. (It may be a bit compulsive, but I have to say I like it. Wishing strangers well is not always just a sham.) Laura moans as though she really needs God's hand, then turns to the audience as though we were a mirror. (The gleam in her eyes as they fix on us makes me want to bolt and run.) "Lord, whatever you want me to look like, show me!"

Then she suddenly rips the veil. "How many of you have had your colors done?"

On to salvation of another kind: an overweight, plain-faced women named Patti is invited to come up and be told whether she is a Winter, Spring, Summer, or Autumn. "By working *with* what God has already done," Laura theorizes, "by working with color, we can work with your natural skin tones and with your hair color." The more virginal, priggish part of me is relieved that we're back in the realm of the infomercial and out of the sacred fire. While Patti is having scarves of different colors flipped around her face, two other women are brought up to the altar. Gina flips one candidate around in a barber's chair so that we see only her back. "I'd like you to meet Barbara." Holding the nape of Barbara's neck possessively, Gina asks the audience whether we agree that she should "cut and shape it a bit." "This is really sexy," I write in my notes. It's also more than a little sadomasochistic. Barbara's eyes are on the floor, and she's so pale and passive that she might be on the end of Gina's leash. Meanwhile, at stage right, Dawn, a congregation member who's been the owner of a "Danbury day spa and makeup and hair salon called Dawn's Pizazz for fifteen years, thank God," gestures authoritatively with her hairbrush at a third candidate/victim. "This is Pamela. She hasn't had her hair done for some time, and we're going to take it to her shoulders and make her look perky!"

Yet the styling-conversions are the least frightening part of the Total Woman experience. Though the three-ring circus setup verges on the humiliating, the makeovers themselves turn out to be rather beautiful expressions of Laura, Dawn, and even dominatrix Gina's love for other women. Even when the advice is wrong (in *my* opinion, which turns out to be far stronger on these matters than I could have ever imagined), the words that go with them are so nurturing as to make the actual look of the frilly blouse-bow or bad bangs beside the point. "She looks so good," Laura says about a middle-aged woman in an unremarkable beige pantsuit. "I think she's got a right color on. But I want to change her earrings. She looks better with the drop than the square, 'cause it elongates her face."

She's what my therapist might sound like if my therapist offered makeup tips: a tender counselor, warm and affirming even when exhorting a change of course. ("You look lovely. But I think you should wear a bolder lipstick.") Laura decks out a sixty-year-old black lady in a squat black hat that's completely wrong for her, makes her look like a duck. "Ain't she elegant?" Laura exclaims. "She just looks so pretty!" She definitely looks lovable, and so we hoot our appreciation for this lady, ridiculous hat and all. It's a touching moment, and I get the idea that no matter what clothes or hairstyle I was wearing, if I were up there Laura would think me pretty, too.

Her advice to the group is just as warmly empathetic. We all have in our closets, Laura says, items that we know we'll never wear without the right accessories. A floral dress that screams pink pumps, say, or a black dress you know you will never wear without the big gold belt that would make it look divine. "So when we get our extra money, ladies, what do we do? We go *buy* those pink pumps, that gold belt!" What is spiritual guidance, after all, but the exhortation to get hold of whatever pink pumps will bring us to beauty? (If your eye offend you, Laura might tell us, accessorize it. With this half of her heart, Laura would never tell anyone to pluck out their eye, or threaten them with hell, the fundamentalist's version of the despair-soaked landscape where one is ugly forever.)

After a while, I feel like following her around as though she were a mother duck herself. "Vests are wonderful, especially for small-busted women. I've picked vests up at Wal-Mart and Target. . . . Don't think you have to tackle your whole closet at once. So many tasks are much easier to accomplish in increments. When you're shopping, ask yourself: is it my right color?" I jot down some of her advice, which I'm actually going to take when I get home (right colors; "bracelets are wonderful"; flattering outfits for short women). Some of her other advice—costume earrings with detachable, different-colored, mix-and-match magnetic stones—I guess I won't. Regardless of whether the suggestions are good or not, it is *nurturing* to be given advice about inconsequential matters in a loving way— actually, it feels a bit like being groomed by one's mother.

My mother was (and is) very loving to me, but in my family when I was growing up, it was hard to be loved or even groomed in an *inconsequential* way. Nothing was inconsequential for us Minkowitzes. Overwhelming emotion was the order of the day, life-and-death issues were the only ones I knew. In the realm of love, we were brought up to be fundamentalists.

Ambivalence was not right, and neither was inattention. Except for my mother, it was hard for anyone to be capricious or frivolous in our house—she was the sole feminine persona in the family, and she performed her most inconsequential deeds (makeup and clothes and anointing herself with perfume) in a profoundly intense manner. The rest of us hardly performed them at all. We were afraid of her withdrawing her love, which she did pretty frequently, threatening to leave the family and often actually going away for a night or two, to show she meant it. She didn't mean to keep us on tenterhooks that way—I don't *think* she meant to—but my mom herself has always been on tenterhooks of the most painful kind, and nothing we did was ever able to remove them.

It always felt safer to be boring and quiet with her rather than excited; she got upset very easily, and when upset, rageful. Always it felt safer not to seem provocative. Yet sometimes provocation seemed to be required. My father competed for her love with the rest of us, as though he were another Minkowitz child, or we, perhaps, alternate husbands. But though required to some extent by the competition, it still felt dangerous to caper or prance around her, or to deck ourselves out. One reason was that my mother didn't understand a great deal about sexual boundaries. She never touched me sexually, but she talked about her sexual desires constantly, informed us how sexy our clothing was (when I was eleven she confided, giggling, that my new two-tone boots made me look like a dominatrix). She discussed her sex life in detail, demanded that I come into her bath each night and wash her back, walked around the house naked and made us admire her. Her constant questions: "Am I the prettiest mother on the block?" and "Do you love me?" And comparisons, always: she once asked me who I loved more, her or my own best friend. It makes sense that in response, we three children were very solemn and masculine. It was impossible for us to be trivial, inane, vacuous, worldly—that was my mother's sole prerogative, and we did not wish to intrude on her frightening orbit. Except for my mother, therefore, we were completely incapable of utterances like Gina's "The red that I put in my hair is very temporary. Then you just have fun. It's not a major change, but it freshens my look for a new season."

Once we were all at the beach and my mother began to draw a woman's face in enormous leering lipstick on my father's naked belly, while a friend of hers looked on and laughed. I understood that this act of drawing was sexual, and I understood that it was humiliating. My father hated it, and he also liked it, I could tell. I understood that having this face drawn around his navel was a way of making him feminine, and shamed. His wide-open, lipsticked belly button was the mouth. He'd turned bright red and was ceaselessly begging her to stop. I hated watching it, and perhaps I also liked it. ("Makeup" has largely meant this to me, until now.)

As Le Guin writes, "The dance is always danced above the hollow place, above the terrible abyss." In other ways, my mother was a wonderful mother. I remember sitting with her every afternoon with a book and a delicious, expensive sandwich while she reorganized the nursery school library, handing me good books to look at periodically and checking to make sure I was still enjoying my voluptuous tuna salad from the deli. I hardly remember anything as wonderful as the combination of a storybook with a sour pickle and my mother's arm around me. When I was six and my mother started college, she brought me home books about Greek mythology and outrageous science fiction. (I loved the angry picture of Poseidon on the cover of one; that book was one of the most exciting things I've ever read.) She sneaked me into one of her grad school classes, where a world-renowed authority on ancient religion was discussing Zoroastrianism. Then she brought me home his cool translation of *The Epic of Gilgamesh*. My mother nurtured my mind and my enjoyment of it at every possible moment. In the realm of literature and learning, ambivalence, questions, and whimsy were A-OK. She encouraged me to read and write at every turn (but rather surprisingly, never pressured me to do it). Literature wasn't hers, it was ours. She's always encouraged my writing in a purely loving, purely positive way, the way the sun encourages the green grass to grow.

The weirdest thing about the marriage of heaven and hell is that they are, in fact, impossible to separate; the heavenly things I got from my mother will never transcend the hellish part, or vice versa. "Every Harlot was a Virgin once," Blake wrote to God and Satan (whom he said were the same being), "nor canst thou ever change Kate into Nan." My mother is very loving, and very destructive. My father hit me all the time, but was ultimately much less scary because he gave me little. Still, he wept the last time he saw me, because he knew he would never see me again, and I've come to understand, years and years after his death, that he, too, loved me. My hatred of him was more than a simple response to his violence. My soul, like everyone's, is innocent and brutal at the same time; it has great beauty and unbelievable grossness in it. It is vulgar and deathless as Jesus incarnated in a purple scarf, trailing its rayon there on Gina's table while women moan with happiness and anger. As for me, I am noxious and tender as Dawn's assistant, bawling, "This woman told me she didn't have the time for makeup! I said to her, 'You're not *finished* unless your face is done!'"

Grace, the head of this church, suddenly leaps onto the dais, nearly knocking the better parts of me and my parents off the stage. When I see her, I understand abruptly that this church isn't just named after "grace," the Christian blessing of forgiveness. It's also named after *her,* Grace—first and last name—the Singing Evangelist, author of *God's Special Instructions for Dealing with Your Problems.* "Good morning!" she bellows, interrupting several makeovers-in-progress. "I want to let you know that I was not sleeping! I was away this morning, but I'm here now!" Grace speaks the way Jesus does in the overweening Gospel of John, the most frightening, absolutist, and Queer Nation–like of the four. I am the way, the truth, and the life, I am alpha and omega, and except they believe in *me,* none shall enter the kingdom of heaven. Grace looks like Elvira, or like a mad Linda Ronstadt hamming it up on *Canciónes de Mi Padre* (sings a bit like her, too), with flowing black locks and the face and gestures of a medieval conjurer. She's wearing a black-and-white cow-

girl suit in which she looks like Shirley Temple in a ped-
erastic porn spread. And, every eye riveted upon her, she
starts to talk about about herself and her bodily functions
in exquisite detail, as though she were on the cross and
were allowing us, like Thomas, to stick our fingers in the
wound.

"A lot of people say, 'Is Grace sick?' But I'm not! I had
gained weight before and now I've lost it. I was on prednisone for a condition that I had, and the prednisone made
me gain weight." It's a long, rambling story, but Grace
delivers every in and out of it, leaving Laura and Gina
unapplauded and forgotten. "Thank God I've been healed.
I tried all those 'diets that work,' and they didn't. The only
thing that works is the word of God. I've seen people that
lost fifty pounds—I swear to God—I've seen a woman
who lost one hundred pounds *by the word of God!*"
Unlike Gina and Laura, everything out of Grace's mouth is
about sex, power, or her body—one avatar or another of
her own intensity. "These two gals, they were afraid of
moving with the Spirit of God before they came here," she
indicates the visiting evangelists, "but I said, 'Go *ahead
and move!*'" Women squeal at her from the audience. "We
want women to get loose for Jesus! *I say don't worry
about what people think, or what they say. Get on with
Jesus!*

"When I was five years old, I had an abusive father,"
Grace continues, "and he took me out in the ocean on his
shoulders, and said, 'If you don't come up, I'm leaving you
there.' He threw me in and he did not pick me up!" But for
her birthday last week, her friends and family took her for
a ride on a "Wave Runner, that's like a motorcycle on the

water, and I heard God say to me, '*You will never drown. The floods will never drown you.*'" Listening to her, I rather wish they had. Every eye is on her, and almost all the women in the room look like they would obey Grace if she asked them to jump off a cliff, perhaps telling them that the air would never refuse to hold them up. At her monthly Miracle Service, Grace tells us, a miracle happens "every single time"—including the healing of "cancer, arthritis, multiple sclerosis, deafness . . ." Says her book jacket, "When Grace prays,"—with a big flower in her hair and an unbearably loud ditty on her lips—"miracles happen."

※

After lunch—where I hear the women at the next table over discussing "the fear" and "the flesh" and "the embarrassment" that take over when you want to let God in—Laura resumes the stage to enact a ritual she'd described to me on the phone as "me standing before you and undressing, so that you can know who Christ is." Thankfully she wasn't being literal. In the afternoon half of the program, which Laura calls "the spiritual part" as contrasted with the "lighthearted" "glamour part" of the A.M., the nicest Total Woman's intimate problems are revealed to us.

Audiences sometimes hate it when you reveal your intimate problems, but I think it's all a matter of delivery. Me, I'm absolutely fond of Laura's intimate problems—sweet, bathetic, and a little surreal, like the problems of Minnie Mouse, or the painful difficulties of Kelly and Donna, the blond best friends on *90210*. At least that's how Laura presents them. "You saw the glamour part this morning. You saw, hopefully, how some of you are gonna be better, smarter shoppers. Now, the reason why." A nun "had told my parents I was a slow learner—maybe borderline retarded." She holds up a thorny flower stem that has no buds and shows it to us. "I remember feeling so outcasted. . . . I felt so dumb and so stupid, and I went through school and made *D*'s and *F*'s.

"I thought that with me being a slow learner, if I could just find a man in my life, it would be whole and complete." But that didn't happen. "I would date a man, get bored, and leave him, and it wouldn't fill the hole that we all have before we come to Jesus Christ." So Laura Tucker got married twice, and "was with other men intimately," some of whom she slept with without ever knowing their names. The turning point came when she "got into aerobics, and took a job at a health spa." There, she met "a beautiful girl named Ellen. Ellen had a love, and I wanted that love. I said, 'I want what you have,' and Ellen began to share with me about Jesus." Laura holds up a single rose amid a bunch of thorns.

"One day when I was managing this health club, a man came up to me and said, 'If you were going to die today, do you believe you would go to Heaven?' It made me really uncomfortable. I wanted him to leave me alone. But thank God for persistent people! I believe now that it was God, because several of the men at the health club that day, I had been with intimately. . . . Little by little, the Lord nudged me." Baby's breath is added to the rose and thorns.

"I met another man. I was managing another health spa, and he wanted to open up a tan spa. So we talked quite often. And he was quite older. . . . Little by little, the more time that I spent in his tan spa, the more I was attracted to him. We got married and opened up a shop called the Body Boutique. . . . So then I began to see the results from my prayers. I had my facial license, we had an aerobics studio, it was a full-service shop. Everything but hair." More roses.

But although Phil was a Christian, he "took a gun one day and shot himself. . . . They found him by the side of the road." He left a note saying: "the pressure has gotten too much for me." (More thorns.) Laura prayed and prayed, and "two words came to me . . . *Total Woman.*" They were not taken, Laura says, from Marabel Morgan's famous 1975 book by the same name, the one that told Christian women how to be ultrastimulating sex slaves and greet their husbands at the door dressed only in Saran Wrap. ("The book is totally different from what our concept is," Laura says emphatically, although "when I read it, I was really touched by it.") Laura met another man, and that man "is my husband now. I said, 'I believe the Lord has called me to ministry and given me the words *Total Woman!* He's called me to ministry in North Carolina!'" The new husband was remarkably compliant with the Lord's desire that they move to a different state. Once there, seeing Christian women on TV who looked dowdy, Laura volunteered her makeup and accessorizing services to the local Christian station.

"After a while, God was saying to me. 'I have called you out. I want you to be *in front* of the camera.'" Tinsel now bedecks the roses and the baby's breath. After Gina joined the show, "our ratings picked up even more."

The tone of this testimony has been light and unpresuming throughout—the very thing that gives it charm. But Laura abruptly shifts gears as she realizes that the afternoon is passing and no one has manifested the Spirit yet. She begins to cry out, "If there is any guilt or shame upon you this day, I command it to go!" Laura wants us to express something more chaotic than her own story, something uncontrollable, more like Grace. She asks "anyone who has been moved by what she's said" to run up front and pluck a rose, but the crowd is uncharacteristically shy. Because no one comes up to be swept away by rosy Jesus ("He's the Rose of Sharon! Jesus is called the Rose of Sharon!" Laura's crying to us), she turns to a simple command, a surefire charisma-getter: "All the mothers, come up here!"

Perhaps half of the crowd goes up in front of the stage, as Laura starts praying in tongues that sound like Elvish: *"Thalioso solalamine . . . io bakalliososo, basolame."* And perhaps a little Greek, Spanish, Basque and Portuguese mixed in—musical, nasal, unearthly, the way I imagine women sounded when they worshipped ecstatically at Eleusis. The crowd by the stage takes up the same syllables, and women begin to touch each other. ("Kiss me lovely one, with your sea salt" is what the translation sounds like to me.) I haven't mentioned how many of the crowd look like lesbians, but my people, or at least women willing to be taken for us, are certainly represented in this hall. An arm-muscled hunk in a tank top and jeans grips another beautiful woman in the row in front of me, and a goofy smile appears on my face. They pray together and chant softly. Is this what the Michigan Womyn's Music Festival is like? I've always been too scared to go.

One woman plays drums on stage: Mary, a butch young woman with no makeup who'd volunteered drolly for the very last makeover ("I need all the help I can get!"), bangs them like she had a crowd of 150 eager women staring at her hands and dancing to her music with abandon. Soon, she does. "Let my people go!" Laura Tucker calls out. "Let my people be set free!" Others call out wise-sounding and self-consciously "biblical" or "prophetic" statements, reminding me of people speaking from the floor of my favorite agape-filled community group of all time, ACT UP. "Verily, verily, it will come to you!" "Lord God, we will never . . ." "This is the time of test . . ."

People start to be "slain in the spirit," falling back with abandon into other people's arms. Others rush up behind them, to be sure to be there when they fall. I have to say this is one of the most beautiful things that I have ever seen. Perhaps it's the trust, the openness? I've gone on smiling goofily for the past twenty minutes, without meaning to. I am being *me,* now, not playing a role—and I can see how easy it would be to choose this answering joy, this present ecstasy, as a way of life.

"Anyone who has a word, come up here!" Laura shouts. This means nonmothers can now join in the all-embracing group warmth, too. Women are known for being extravagantly open to one another—"merging," lesbians call it—and these women from Grace 'N Vessels are going to merge before my very eyes, hugely, publicly, and unashamedly. I am envious. Why don't I join them in the warm bath of all-embracing love, why didn't I volunteer for a makeover in front of everyone? While Mary drums to a sexy, jazzy beat, Alicia sings, over and over, "Let my mouth be filled with your praise." I see her mouth, and my mouth, being filled with the ecstatic body parts that might be said to constitute someone's "praise."

Laura wants to make the circle even bigger. "Anyone who feels called to minister, come up here!" she calls out. About twenty more women step forward. It's at this point that Grace approaches from the sidelines and begins to do her thing. She lines women up like dominoes in front of her and spookily raises her hands, "conjuring" them to fall. Soon, they are all waiting on her command, not falling till she gives the signal. The very butchest woman in the crowd, a tall *bullvon* in an NCAA Final Four shirt, has been jumping to position herself behind women for an hour, as if it were her personal responsibility to hold up female beings when they fall. "NCAA" questions Grace with her eyes whether she should stand behind a certain woman, but Grace rather rudely and abruptly signals no. Grace wants another woman to fall first, and motions NCAA and the other catchers to stand behind her own picked candidate instead. This isn't just "openness," but something at once more directed, and more hysterical; like a military game, or a torment-game from children's parties, a sort of commanded trust.

Gina begins to do the same thing as Grace. She doesn't raise her hands like a bandleader, but comes closer and lays them on women, pushing their backs gently as though she were burping babies. There is discernible pressure in a little scene going on right in front of me, with Gina wreaking her energies on a very young woman who she says is a recent survivor of satanic abuse. The girl was rescued from a family of satanists, Gina says. She grasps the little redheaded survivor from the front while NCAA and several others press upon her from the back, to the girl's intermittent moans. "Pain! Shame! Go!" Gina cries laconically as all the women stroke her. The buildup and the pressure go on for almost too long—*this feels like a delayed orgasm* I write in my pad, and all of us, me included, are focused on the young woman and whether she'll fall off that metaphoric cliff. When she still doesn't go to pieces in spite of all their efforts, Gina hugs her quietly. "Rejection should go," she murmurs tenderly, as though she were comforting a boyfriend who was impotent.

This rite is both beautiful and frightening. And ugly. Many women put their hands on one frail, blond girl, looking as though they really believed they were putting God's spirit on her. Whatever the benefits, I wouldn't want to receive God's spirit through someone else's active mediation. I've been taken to heaven by my friends and even by my lovers, but they took me there without being fully cognizant of it. They did not have the smarmy notion that one person can ever be fully responsible for another's encounter with the holy; they just took me there by being them. I've been taken there, in the same unconscious way, at the Promise Keepers' rally by beautiful strangers, and by the Reverend Fred Phelps, who carries signs that say that GOD HATES FAGS and who would rather have died than knowingly bring me someplace nice. Never through any intervention as deliberate and hectic as this, the predatory rescue-mission of women who thought they had a direct connection to the godhead and I didn't.

(After consummation, apparently, the intercessors' interest fades. "They get you up too fast," one elderly woman coming back to my row gripes in a low voice to a friend. "They don't let you lie down.")

And the language of the ritual gets more inflamed and sexual by the second:

"Fill her, Lord Jesus!" Gina cries, as the throng surrounds a fifty-five-year-old black woman. "*Fill her! Fill her! Fill her, Lord!* Fill her right now!" It's like a gang rape in a porn novel: The woman grunts out animal noises and bucks against her holy assailants, finally collapsing with a sob of "*Yes,* Lord! *yes! yes! yes!*" (Another grandma had been the star attraction just minutes previous. For her, Gina had pleaded in the spontaneous rhyming style you will see in books like *Horny Lonely Housewife:* "Give her the fire, the fire, the fire! That is her heart's desire!")

Of another woman: "She's gonna say *Holy ghost, holy ghost, holy ghost,* take the reins to her life!" Of another: "You're gonna stay and melt her, melt her, melt her, Lord Jesus, *melt her* . . ." Women pitch and totter as Gina invites Jesus to enter them ("In Jesus' name! In Jesus' name! Oh God, fill her, fill her, fill her, fill her, *in Jesus' name!*"), invokes S/M imagery ("Oh, I pray you bring the harnesses upon her, Lord!"), and makes teasing noises like a coquette ("*Ohhh* God! *Ohhh* Holy Spirit!").

But it is Grace who carries the erotic banner furthest. She hoots for our attention, comes to the center of the room, and starts singing at the top of her lungs, "*Ain't nobody do me like Jesus!*" She gets the audience to respond antiphonally, "No, / Ain't nobody do me like Jesus," while a teenager kicks her legs like a Rockette to the beat. Grace grabs two of the youngest children in the audience, girls about five or six years old, and makes them dance and sing with her in a little circle, very like those nubile bump-and-grind playground dances little girls have been learning to do for some years now. The girls smile unctuously and warble, *"Ain't nobody do me like Jesus! Can't nobody do me like Jesus!"* and I feel abruptly nauseous. I flee to the bathroom.

I'm a prig. Yes. I overreact to all interactions with children. (I sometimes overreact to plain old sex, as well.) What Grace is doing is gross, but not so gross that the world is going to end and I have to torture her immediately with a bread knife on the floor of her own church.

It's a welcome refuge, the ladies' room. Grace 'N Vessels' bathroom has flowers stenciled on every stall door; a stained-glass window; a beautiful full-length mirror; unimpeachable cleanliness; abundant paper towels; even hand cream. Without question, it's one of the most beautiful bathrooms I have ever seen. Do women have to flee in here very often to escape the intensity of the services? The Carry Nation inside me finds it easy to console herself with the immaculate tiles, the dried-flower arrangements. She's becoming chilly so she won't burn up.

Do you blame her? The tight-lipped prig inside me is directly connected to the exhibitionistic trollop.

The Maenad who rips living people's flesh is the same person as the girl who hides in the bathroom. The one rips flesh for the same chilly reason that the other one hides. "Enough! or Too much," Blake wrote. And: "You can never know what is enough until you know what is more than enough." I have had more than enough; it has stuck in my throat. I am still trying to learn to have enough. The prig in me is the same being as the one who thinks that only sex is holy, that I am worthless and filthy without the purifying sacred fire. The one who holds back is the same girl who explodes.

On a chintz-covered table in the church's anteroom is a gold-framed certificate stating the church's rules. The document says that Grace 'N Vessels is not responsible for any injuries caused by being slain in the spirit: "Your participation is at your own choosing and at your own risk." It also says that cameras and tape recorders are forbidden, "because of the intensity of these acts." But coming to services means you give the *church* permission to record your ecstasies; Grace 'N Vessels is entitled to "use your image and use your voice." Even more porn bells there. I'm glad that all I did in this crowd scene was to smile a lot and clap my hands.

Many charismatic Christians get just as hot and bothered as I do about the sexual subtext of their services. "Pentecostals are very sensitive to such [charges] and extraordinarily careful to prevent sexual hanky-panky under cover of prayer," writes leftist religion scholar Harvey Cox in his famously uncritical study of Pentecostalism, *Fire from Heaven.* In many charismatic churches, men only "catch" men and women only "catch" women, in order to forestall heterosexual passion during services. This doesn't of course, prevent lesbian eroticism from emerging in the heat of the uncontrollable union with the divine. Somehow, in a religious movement notably dedicated to the suppression of female and gay and lesbian sexuality, one of the most common religious rites involves women writhing on the floor with their arms around each other, shaking uncontrollably as they beg each other to be "melted." Perhaps it's no accident that evangelicals' name for their relationship with other believers is the Body.

I'm not surprised that eros feels so overwhelming to them that they have to go to anti-sexual churches to express it. Until recently, it has often felt that overwhelming to me, too. Even in the backroom of the Labia Lounge, my own sacristy for the fire from heaven, I would sometimes get as overwrought as Jonathan Edwards trembling at the hideous majesty of God. The Labia Lounge, where all you had to do was ask and you would receive, where you would knock and the door would open, was a much safer space than a relationship, where the fire would be that much more searing and excruciating. Where I might hang naked on a cross for someone for God knows how long . . . experiencing the unbearable feeling of connection, the horrible dangers of trust. But even in the comfort-giving Lounge itself, sometimes the heady smell of the place, the constant sex going on around me (and on me), the general sensory overload of eight women packed in a tiny room in the dark stimulating each other, with New Wave music pulsating in from the bar . . . would throw me off my feet. . . . Sometimes I would literally have to take a breather, go outside and breathe my own, separate air.

The backroom was the one place where the idea of the Goddess has ever felt comfortable to me. Worshipping the Goddess is exactly what it felt like we were doing there—making each other feel good in the warm, sweet dark; loving the bodies of every woman in the room—fat, fatter, and slim (I remember marveling at the goodness of fat, in that dark room); refraining from hating the marshy genitals of women the way everyone in this society, male and female, has been taught to do. We hate women's bodies because they remind us frighteningly of love. They remind us of victims because love makes us open; slips in always where we are most vulnerable; is risky always and eternally, on both sides, unomnipotent, imperfectable, and can never be made safe.

Unsurprisingly, apart from the backroom I've always hated the notion of female deities. Part of the reason I react the way I do to Grace and Gina is because they're *women*, and therefore, excessively easy for me to hate. (Men, however voracious, are seldom described as looking "ravenous.") If Grace were just as overbearing and she were a man, I wouldn't like her, but I wouldn't want to disembowel her slowly, to music, while eating creamy bonbons the way I do. (I'm sorry if I offend, but I did say I was a misogynist. I am trying very hard not to be one.) Then again, the quality I believe I hate most of all in Grace and Gina is their boundarylessness, a characteristically female quality (perhaps *the* characteristically female quality). It repels me more than the worst characteristically male qualities, including violence and rape—which are themselves, come to think of it, also forms of boundarylessness, just forms that come unmixed with love.

—Repels me more, until right now. For I am changing even as I write this; on my desk are two small candles in the form of sushi, the most beautiful foodstuffs I've ever put inside my mouth. One offers fertile orange roe, nearly spilling over with it; the other is raw flesh of shrimp, silky, almost immaterial. Sex has been changing for me in a way beyond my comprehension, and the only response that I can undertake is praise. It has not been frightening for me lately—a staggering experience, rather like stumbling into a garden when you expected a consuming holy furnace. The garden is different; there is so much in it I've never experienced.

ß

I've had to disarm myself to get inside this land. I took off my weapons, and my incense too. And as my feet dipped in the velvety grass I could see that there was no redeemer. No enslaver. Only other people.

I approached them with great joy.

Afterword

When I learned that nothing could save me, I discovered nothing could damn me, either.

The subject of this book has been the Other, on many levels—the enemy, the beloved, and also everything in our own lives that we would like to externalize. Pain, evil, our past histories . . . and also holiness, the numinous grace we often cannot bear to see within ourselves.

For everything I had fled from was a part of me. And all I had run after was a part of me, too. Grace, Gina, my mother . . . and the callipygian Venus herself.

Sex was inside me whether or not I interacted with the Other.

Love was inside me, too.

There were fountains of both that would not run dry . . .

In the end, I discovered there were other reasons for seeking out the Other than to substitute for a debt that can never be paid (like a burnt offering), or deliver me.

᭬

Nothing can save me from the dangers of the other, but nothing can ever take away the other's beauty, either.